THE
EVERYDAY
GUIDE TO...
THE PSALMS

THE EVERYDAY GUIDE TO...
THE PSALMS

PAMELA McQUADE

HUMBLECREEK
INSPIRATION FOR LIFE

© 2005 by Barbour Publishing, Inc.

ISBN 1-59310-728-5

All scripture quotations, unless otherwise noted, are taken from the King James Version of the Bible.

Published by Humble Creek, P.O. Box 719, Uhrichsville, Ohio 44683

Printed in the United States of America.
5 4 3 2 1

Contents

Introduction

Many Christians say the Psalms are their favorite book of the Bible or at least contain some of their favorite passages. Perhaps that's because the Psalms provide an intimate view of the godly life as experienced by those who both struggled with it and were very successful at it.

The Psalms speak in colorful, poetic language, relating to daily experience. They often speak in word pictures, graphic verbal descriptions that put an image in your head and make you relate more personally to them. When David says the Lord is his shepherd, you immediately relate to God's protection and care.

Alas, the entire text of the book of Psalms is not reproduced here, for space reasons. Neither has every psalm been included. But I'd like to encourage you to read the whole Bible, including all the Psalms. Purchase a Bible or request one from a Bible society. You may even access the scriptures online and read each complete psalm. Enjoy them whole. When you have covered a few weeks in this volume, you will begin to understand even the chapters not covered here.

The book of Psalms consists of five smaller books, compiled at different times in the history of the Jews. The psalms in each reflect the situation in Israel—the first book, containing many psalms written by King David, at times closely follows his experiences. The second book was added around the time of David's son Solomon. Books three and four, written before the Jews' exile to Babylon, mirror the turmoil of that age and emphasize the need to rely on God for stability. Book five collects psalms from the time after the Israelites returned to their land.

In many Bibles, at the head of most of the psalms is a superscription that may describe the authorship, the situation in which it was written, or give some musical direction. They have not been included here, although I have tried to provide the important information about each in the text.

The Psalms often follow a format in which the psalmist describes a problem in the first few verses, considers it in light of humanity and God, comes to a point of faith and praise, and ends up worshiping God. This does not show lack of faith, but a mature consideration of how life and faith interact. Frequently psalmists cry out for God to help the needy or helpless. We understand their concern, since we do the same thing when we ask, "Where was God when such-and-such tragedy occurred?" For the psalmists, there was no doubt God would act to save His people, even if they waited long for their rescue.

Often the Psalms compare the lifestyle of the wicked, who do not know and serve God, with those who love and live for him. David speaks of his own innocence, in comparison to the wicked. When psalmists speak of their own lack of sin, they do not claim personal perfection. Clearly, from the needs they brought before their Lord, they were more than aware of their own inability to be pure. But their hearts desired to live to honor God and do His will lifelong. These are the hallmarks of faithful Christians, though they may experience times of failure. No one other than God is consistently perfect. But those who have experienced God's salvation daily seek to become more like Him.

As you study these pages, I hope the psalms will impact your life. That is why each psalm includes a section with questions for reflection. No one fully understands the scriptures until they influence daily living. I hope these will help that happen.

PAMELA MCQUADE

WEEK ONE

Introduction

The Psalms, the hymnbook of the Bible, are all written in poetry. These poems cover a diverse range of topics: Some are straightforward praise of God; some are prayers for help, rescue, or thanksgiving; and others are diatribes against the acts of evil men who take advantage of the faithful. But all show a deep faith in the Almighty, who controls all the earth and eternity.

This week we will become acquainted with David, who wrote many of the psalms. This founder of Israel's line of kings did not have a simple life, though he started as a shepherd, looking after his father's herd. As a young man, the prophet Samuel anointed David king, signifying that God had chosen him to rule. But the previous king, Saul, remained on the throne, denying God's authority. For years, David battled for the position in which God placed him. (You can read about Saul's and David's histories in the Bible's books of 1 and 2 Samuel.) Many psalms reflect their struggle, and perhaps because it was so much a part of his life, David often uses military language to speak of both physical and spiritual battles. But David also deeply understood both God's nature and human failure and has a great sensitivity to the emotions that are part of faith and doubt.

All the psalms reflect an extraordinary understanding of people's hearts and minds, including those things that drive them to evil or devotion to God. Clearly, the Holy Spirit gave the men who wrote the Bible inspiration beyond their own understanding. Scripture reaches into hearts and touch lives in a way no human words can.

The psalmists draw a clear distinction, which is sometimes uncomfortable to us, between those who love God and those who don't. They are not afraid to describe someone as "wicked" or "pagan." The God who sees into each person's heart knows who really has faith in him and who is simply pretending. If we do not believe, we need to admit that, go to God with our sin, and ask Him for forgiveness. There is no other way to faith.

The Spirit works in many ways in the Bible. Amazingly, though he lived centuries before Jesus, David, who began the messianic kingly line, speaks often about the Messiah who was to come (Psalm 2 is one example). Messianic psalms usually describe two kings at the same time: the earthly king of Israel and the King and Savior who was yet to come, Jesus. They may also refer to Jesus' Second Coming, prophesied in both the Old and New Testaments. This can lead to some confusion of understanding, until readers comprehend this two-at-the-same-time kind of reference and apply it properly. But the Spirit also works in our hearts, if we know Christ, to help us comprehend. All we need do is submit ourselves to Him, ask for help, and accept the truths He reveals.

May God work in these studies to help that understanding begin, because nothing is better than knowing Him and knowing Him well.

Psalm 1

1 Blessed is the man that walketh not in the counsel of the ungodly, nor standeth in the way of sinners, nor sitteth in the seat of the scornful.

2 But his delight is in the law of the Lord; and in his law doth he meditate day and night.

3 And he shall be like a tree planted by the rivers of water, that bringeth forth his fruit in his season; his leaf also shall not wither; and whatsoever he doeth shall prosper.

4 The ungodly are not so: but are like the chaff which the wind driveth away.

5 Therefore the ungodly shall not stand in the judgment, nor sinners in the congregation of the righteous.

6 For the Lord knoweth the way of the righteous: but the way of the ungodly shall perish.

Psalm 2

1 Why do the nations rage, And the peoples meditate a vain thing?

2 The kings of the earth set themselves, And the rulers take counsel together, Against Jehovah, and against his anointed, saying,

3 Let us break their bonds asunder, And cast away their cords from us.

4 He that sitteth in the heavens will laugh: The Lord will have them in derision.

5 Then will he speak unto them in his wrath, And vex them in his sore displeasure:

6 Yet I have set my king upon my holy hill of Zion.

7 I will tell of the decree: Jehovah said unto me, Thou art my son; This day have I begotten thee.

8 Ask of me, and I will give thee the nations for thine inheritance, And the uttermost parts of the earth for thy possession.

9 Thou shalt break them with a rod of iron; Thou shalt dash them in pieces like a potter's vessel.

10 Now therefore be wise, O ye kings: Be instructed, ye judges of the earth.

11 Serve Jehovah with fear, And rejoice with trembling.

12 Kiss the son, lest he be angry, and ye perish in the way, For his wrath will soon be kindled. Blessed are all they that take refuge in him.

For Your Information

"Blessed": happy. Those who love God receive good things from Him.

"Man": In the King James Bible "man" is often a generic word to refer to both sexes.

The "law": God's commandments, the Bible.

"Chaff": useless debris, left over from grain threshing. It is light and easily blown away.

"Messiah" (Hebrew) and "Christ" (Greek): the Old Testament and New Testament words meaning "anointed one." Both the line of David and Jesus were anointed, or chosen, by God.

"Heathen": pagan nations or those who do not know God.

"Imagine a vain thing": engage in worthless plots.

"Holy hill of Zion": Jerusalem.

"Son": the anointed one.

"Kiss": sign of submission.

Psalm 1

The first psalm describes two kinds of people—those who love God and live in His way and "the ungodly," who live by their own rules and ignore God. The blessed, or righteous, person seeks to live a lifestyle pleasing to God and receives His approval and good things—both spiritual and physical—from His hand.

Scripture is not shy about describing people as being wicked or evil. Not many details appear about the lifestyle of the evil ones, since the Word does not glorify this behavior, but it warns of judgment to come for those who continue on this path.

Finally, the psalm gives a balanced assessment of the end of each lifestyle: While God watches over His people, those who deny Him will die.

• Compare the godly and ungodly: What do the godly avoid? What do they do? What blessings do they receive?

• How does this Psalm describe the ungodly? What kind of life do they live? What do they receive?

• What kind of life do you want to have? Which lifestyle will get it for you?

Psalm 2

This is a Messianic psalm. Though it describes the warfare of King David, who is attacked by the nations that surround him, it simultaneously describes the battles of the end times, when Christ comes in His glory and overthrows the wicked.

Ungodly rulers rebel against God and His earthly representative, resulting in temporal and spiritual warfare. The king's fight against his worldly enemies reflects God's battle against the spiritually rebellious ones who don't accept the Messiah's coming eternal reign.

• How do Christians engage in physical warfare? Spiritual battle? If you are part of a struggle today, how can you know that you are following God's will?

• After reviewing Psalm 1 and this psalm, can you give a description of the attitudes that prevailed with David and God's enemies? Why to people rebel against God's rule? What does God promise will happen to them? How can they avoid this?

Psalm 3

1 Lord, how are they increased that trouble me! many are they that rise up against me.

2 Many there be which say of my soul, There is no help for him in God. Selah.

3 But thou, O Lord, art a shield for me; my glory, and the lifter up of mine head.

4 I cried unto the Lord with my voice, and he heard me out of his holy hill. Selah.

5 I laid me down and slept; I awaked; for the Lord sustained me.

6 I will not be afraid of ten thousands of people, that have set themselves against me round about.

7 Arise, O Lord; save me, O my God: for thou hast smitten all mine enemies upon the cheek bone; thou hast broken the teeth of the ungodly.

8 Salvation belongeth unto the Lord: thy blessing is upon thy people. Selah.

Psalm 4

1 Hear me when I call, O God of my righteousness: thou hast enlarged me when I was in distress; have mercy upon me, and hear my prayer.

2 O ye sons of men, how long will ye turn my glory into shame? how long will ye love vanity, and seek after leasing? Selah.

3 But know that the Lord hath set apart him that is godly for himself: the Lord will hear when I call unto him.

4 Stand in awe, and sin not: commune with your own heart upon your bed, and be still. Selah.

5 Offer the sacrifices of righteousness, and put your trust in the Lord.

6 There be many that say, Who will shew us any good? Lord, lift thou up the light of thy countenance upon us.

7 Thou hast put gladness in my heart, more than in the time that their corn and their wine increased.

8 I will both lay me down in peace, and sleep: for thou, Lord, only makest me dwell in safety.

For Your Information

"Selah": a word of uncertain meaning, probably indicating a musical interlude.

"Smitten": hit.

"Shield": a picture of protection.

"Hast enlarged me": have given me relief.

"Vanity": worthless things.

"Shew": show.

"Their corn and their wine increased": indicates a time of prosperity.

Psalm 3

King David, who wrote this psalm, knew what it meant to face foes. He wrote these verses after his son Absalom overthrew him as king of Israel (2 Samuel 15–18).

In the midst of trial, David responds faithfully. Instead of merely bemoaning his son's treachery, the king places his trust in the Lord who gave him his position. He describes God as his protector and uplifter, and waking or sleeping he need not fear. David asks God to deliver him from his enemies, striking the winning blow.

• Psalms 1–3 describe "the ungodly" or "heathen." What have you learned about hem in these psalms?

• What have you learned about God's attitude towards those who follow Him? How does He protect them?

Psalm 4

David sends many cries for help God's way. Like us, he was very concerned that God would hear and take action in his behalf. So he calls all people to seek God in moments of distress, instead of turning from Him in discouragement. Trusting faith will bring them joy, no matter what their situation, and they will rest in peace, with God as their protector.

- David faced many trials and was tempted to doubt God. Some of his failures of faith, described in 2 Samuel, were immense. But to the day he died, David believed. Have you faced trials and failures? Have you turned to God again and again?

- When you face times of trial, what advice would David give you? How would you respond?

Psalm 5

1 Give ear to my words, O Lord, consider my meditation.

2 Hearken unto the voice of my cry, my king, and my God: for unto thee will I pray.

3 My voice shalt thou hear in the morning, O Lord; in the morning will I direct my prayer unto thee, and will look up.

4 For thou art not a God that hath pleasure in wickedness: neither shall evil dwell with thee.

5 The foolish shall not stand in thy sight: thou hatest all workers of iniquity.

6 Thou shalt destroy them that speak leasing: the Lord will abhor the bloody and deceitful man.

7 But as for me, I will come into thy house in the multitude of thy mercy: and in thy fear will I worship toward thy holy temple.

8 Lead me, O Lord, in thy righteousness because of mine enemies; make thy way straight before my face.

9 For there is no faithfulness in their mouth; their inward part is very wickedness; their throat is an open sepulchre; they flatter with their tongue.

10 Destroy thou them, O God; let them fall by their own counsels; cast them out in the multitude of their transgressions; for they have rebelled against thee.

11 But let all those that put their trust in thee rejoice: let them ever shout for joy, because thou defendest them: let them also that love thy name be joyful in thee.

12 For thou, Lord, wilt bless the righteous; with favour wilt thou compass him as with a shield.

Psalm 6

1 O Lord, rebuke me not in thine anger, neither chasten me in thy hot displeasure.

2 Have mercy upon me, O Lord; for I am weak: O Lord, heal me; for my bones are vexed.

3 My soul is also sore vexed: but thou, O Lord, how long?

4 Return, O Lord, deliver my soul: oh save me for thy mercies' sake.

5 For in death there is no remembrance of thee: in the grave who shall give thee thanks?

6 I am weary with my groaning; all the night make I my bed to swim; I water my couch with my tears.

7 Mine eye is consumed because grief; it waxeth old because of all mine enemies.

8 Depart from me, all ye workers of iniquity; for the Lord hath heard the voice of my weeping.

9 The Lord hath heard my supplication; the Lord will receive my prayer.

10 Let all mine enemies be ashamed and sore vexed: let them return and be ashamed suddenly.

For Your Information

"Hearken": listen.

"Wickedness": evil.

"Leasing": lies.

"Temple": place of worship.

"Sepulchre": tomb.

"Thy name": God's name symbolizes His character.

"Compass": surround.

"Vexed": in agony, suffering.

David sinned, yet God called him "a man after mine own heart" (Acts 13:22). Though he erred, David trusted in God and repented, changing his actions and lifestyle.

Psalm 5

Like Psalm 1, this psalm compares the wicked person and the one who serves God, however imperfectly. After humbly asking God to listen to his prayer, David describes sins that stop God's ears (verses 4–6); God cannot listen to those who do not love and serve Him. The psalmist, an example of the godly man, indicates his willingness to serve his Lord and outlines the blessings offered to those who live for God.

- Have you ever felt God was not listening to you? Does David have a prescription for your problem? What is it?

- Have you repented for the sin in your life and asked God to help you live for Him? If not, now is a good time to do this.

Psalm 6
David recognized the weakness of his own body and his spiritual need for God's mercy as he penned this psalm. In it he asks for healing, and even asks God to save him from death (v. 5). He describes the emotional and physical anguish he experiences, but his agonies turn to praise as God responds with mercy and puts his enemies to route by healing the king.

- Does David's response to physical affliction strike a chord with you? Have you suffered with illness and feared for you life? Where did you turn in this situation? Where would you turn if doctors failed you?

Psalm 7

1 O Lord my God, in thee do I put my trust: save me from all them that persecute me, and deliver me:

2 Lest he tear my soul like a lion, rending it in pieces, while there is none to deliver.

3 O Lord my God, if I have done this; if there be iniquity in my hands;

4 If I have rewarded evil unto him that was at peace with me; (yea, I have delivered him that without cause is mine enemy:)

5 Let the enemy persecute my soul, and take it; yea, let him tread down my life upon the earth, and lay mine honour in the dust. Selah.

6 Arise, O Lord, in thine anger, lift up thyself because of the rage of mine enemies: and awake for me to the judgment that thou hast commanded.

7 So shall the congregation of the people compass thee about: for their sakes therefore return thou on high.

8 The Lord shall judge the people: judge me, O Lord, according to my righteousness, and according to mine integrity that is in me.

9 Oh let the wickedness of the wicked come to an end; but establish the just: for the righteous God trieth the hearts and reins.

10 My defence is of God, which saveth the upright in heart.

God judgeth the righteous, and God is angry with the wicked every day.

12 If he turn not, he will whet his sword; he hath bent his bow, and made it ready.

13 He hath also prepared for him the instruments of death; he ordaineth his arrows against the persecutors.

14 Behold, he travaileth with iniquity, and hath conceived mischief, and brought forth falsehood.

15 He made a pit, and digged it, and is fallen into the ditch which he made.

16 His mischief shall return upon his own head, and his violent dealing shall come down upon his own pate.

17 I will praise the Lord according to his righteousness: and will sing praise to the name of the Lord most high.

For Your Information
"Lest": for fear that.

"Iniquity": guilt, wrongdoing.

"Most High": Sovereign God, the maker of heaven and earth.

"Return thou on high": rule over them from above.

"Upright in heart": pure in heart, without sin.

"Whet": sharpen.

"Travail": toil or childbirth.

"Pate": head.

Psalm 7
Here David asked God to save him from the words of Cush, a now unknown person who may have supported King Saul, David's enemy. The psalmist pleads with God to intervene in their argument, and says he has not done evil. Secure in his own lack of offense, but willing to suffer for his own sins, David requests that God judge each party and punish the wrongdoer. Verses 14–16 describe how evil ones bring wrong down on their own heads.

Finally, David promises he will praise Almighty God, whom he is certain will see him vindicated.

• David is willing to have God punish him, if he has done wrong (verses 3–5). What gave him such confidence? What does this show you about David and his relationship with God?

• Why is the idea of God punishing people so hard to accept today? Does David have a different view of God's justice?

Psalm 9

1 I will praise thee, O Lord, with my whole heart; I will shew forth all thy marvellous works.

2 I will be glad and rejoice in thee: I will sing praise to thy name, O thou most High.

3 When mine enemies are turned back, they shall fall and perish at thy presence.

4 For thou hast maintained my right and my cause; thou satest in the throne judging right.

5 Thou hast rebuked the heathen, thou hast destroyed the wicked, thou hast put out their name for ever and ever.

6 O thou enemy, destructions are come to a perpetual end: and thou hast destroyed cities; their memorial is perished with them.

7 But the Lord shall endure for ever: he hath prepared his throne for judgment.

8 And he shall judge the world in righteousness, he shall minister judgment to the people in uprightness.

9 The Lord also will be a refuge for the oppressed, a refuge in times of trouble.

10 And they that know thy name will put their trust in thee: for thou, Lord, hast not forsaken them that seek thee.

11 Sing praises to the Lord, which dwelleth in Zion: declare among the people his doings.

12 When he maketh inquisition for blood, he remembereth them: he forgetteth not the cry of the humble.

13 Have mercy upon me, O Lord; consider my trouble which I suffer of them that hate me, thou that liftest me up from the gates of death:

14 That I may shew forth all thy praise in the gates of the daughter of Zion: I will rejoice in thy salvation.

15 The heathen are sunk down in the pit that they made: in the net which they hid is their own foot taken.

16 The Lord is known by the judgment which he executeth: the wicked is snared in the work of his own hands. Higgaion. Selah.

17 The wicked shall be turned into hell, and all the nations that forget God.

18 For the needy shall not alway be forgotten: the expectation of the poor shall not perish for ever.

19 Arise, O Lord; let not man prevail: let the heathen be judged in thy sight.

20 Put them in fear, O Lord: that the nations may know themselves to be but men. Selah.

For Your Information

"Heart": symbolic of the spirit, which guides a person's actions.

"Satest": sat.

"Put out": blotted out.

"Daughter of Zion": Jerusalem and its people.

"Higgaion": an unknown term that may be a musical notation.

Psalm 9

Publicly David rejoices that God delivered him and his people. Though we know nothing of the event that fostered this praise, clearly God turned back another nation from harming Israel. Since there is no description of a battle, another catastrophic event may have intervened and stopped the attacker. Whatever happened, it completely destroyed the enemy, and David declares this is God's judgment upon them.

David asks his people to join him in praise (verses 11–12) of their God, who has not forgotten them in their need.

The psalmist, who felt he was near death, asks his Savior to lift him up, so he may praise Him all the more in Jerusalem. He rejoices that his enemies trapped themselves in their own evil, and God took a hand in it. Though the wicked nations forget God and die, He will always remember those who trust in Him. God is truly just.

- David is certain God intervened in his favor, though no battle was fought. What about God's character led him to this conclusion? How well do you know God's character?

- Has disaster been suddenly diverted in your life? How did you explain it at the time? Can you see God at work in your life in that situation?

- Have you ever wanted to claim that God had judged another person's wrongdoing, when they experienced disaster? Why does this claim need to be made carefully? What can happen if it isn't?

Psalm 10

1 Why standest thou afar off, O Lord? why hidest thou thyself in times of trouble?

2 The wicked in his pride doth persecute the poor: let them be taken in the devices that they have imagined.

3 For the wicked boasteth of his heart's desire, and blesseth the covetous, whom the Lord abhorreth.

4 The wicked, through the pride of his countenance, will not seek after God: God is not in all his thoughts.

5 His ways are always grievous; thy judgments are far above out of his sight: as for all his enemies, he puffeth at them.

6 He hath said in his heart, I shall not be moved: for I shall never be in adversity.

7 His mouth is full of cursing and deceit and fraud: under his tongue is mischief and vanity.

8 He sitteth in the lurking places of the villages: in the secret places doth he murder the innocent: his eyes are privily set against the poor.

9 He lieth in wait secretly as a lion in his den: he lieth in wait to catch the poor: he doth catch the poor, when he draweth him into his net.

10 He croucheth, and humbleth himself, that the poor may fall by his strong ones.

11 He hath said in his heart, God hath forgotten: he hideth his face; he will never see it.

12 Arise, O Lord; O God, lift up thine hand: forget not the humble.

13 Wherefore doth the wicked contemn God? he hath said in his heart, Thou wilt not require it.

14 Thou hast seen it; for thou beholdest mischief and spite, to requite it with thy hand: the poor committeth himself unto thee; thou art the helper of the fatherless.

15 Break thou the arm of the wicked and the evil man: seek out his wickedness till thou find none.

16 The Lord is king for ever and ever: the heathen are perished out of his land.

17 Lord, thou hast heard the desire of the humble: thou wilt prepare their heart, thou wilt cause thine ear to hear:

18 To judge the fatherless and the oppressed, that the man of the earth may no more oppress.

For Your Information

"Covetous": greedy.

"Grievous": prospering.

"Puffeth": sneers.

"Privily": secretly.

"Contemn": spurn.

"Requite": repay.

"Fatherless": The Bible frequently commands compassion towards the fatherless (see Exodus 22:22; Deuteronomy 24:7; Psalm 82:3; Zechariah 7:10).

Psalm 10

This psalm is one of thirty-four "orphan" psalms, with no titles at the beginning (called superscriptions) to tell us who wrote them or the occasion on which they were written. According to some scholars, it is possible this is a continuation of Psalm 9.

Like most of us, the psalmist wondered why God didn't always rush in to help people in trouble. He saw evil men harming the innocent, and though he knew God cared and would see justice done, the psalmist ached for it to happen immediately.

Wicked ones hunt down and seek to harm the innocent, entrapping them in evil. The writer deftly outlines the evil thoughts and feelings that lead to such actions. Those who do such things do not expect to be caught or stopped, since God has not acted swiftly against them. But the psalmist calls God to destroy the powers of the wicked man and eradicate evil. He has faith that his God, who hears the humble, will respond. One day, the oppression shall end.

• Have you ever wondered why God did not respond to evil? Has it caused you not to trust in Him? How might the psalmist respond to your doubts? Does oppression eventually end?

Psalm 8

1 O Lord, our Lord, how excellent is thy name in all the earth! who hast set thy glory above the heavens.

2 Out of the mouth of babes and sucklings hast thou ordained strength because of thine enemies, that thou mightest still the enemy and the avenger.

3 When I consider thy heavens, the work of thy fingers, the moon and the stars, which thou hast ordained;

4 What is man, that thou art mindful of him? and the son of man, that thou visitest him?

5 For thou hast made him a little lower than the angels, and hast crowned him with glory and honour.

6 Thou madest him to have dominion over the works of thy hands; thou hast put all things under his feet:

7 All sheep and oxen, yea, and the beasts of the field;

8 The fowl of the air, and the fish of the sea, and whatsoever passeth through the paths of the seas.

9 O Lord our Lord, how excellent is thy name in all the earth!

Psalm 11

1 In the Lord put I my trust: how say ye to my soul, Flee as a bird to your mountain?

2 For, lo, the wicked bend their bow, they make ready their arrow upon the string, that they may privily shoot at the upright in heart.

3 If the foundations be destroyed, what can the righteous do?

4 The Lord is in his holy temple, the Lord's throne is in heaven: his eyes behold, his eyelids try, the children of men.

5 The Lord trieth the righteous: but the wicked and him that loveth violence his soul hateth.

6 Upon the wicked he shall rain snares, fire and brimstone, and an horrible tempest: this shall be the portion of their cup.

7 For the righteous Lord loveth righteousness; his countenance doth behold the upright.

For Your Information

"Set thy glory above the heavens": God set His glory above the created earth.

"Suckling": infant.

"Foundations": of the world.

"Try": judge, examine.

Psalm 8

In this pure praise psalm, David rejoices in the Creator God who made His glory so obvious that even tiny children praise Him. Looking at the world God made, David is amazed, not the least at the fact that He even considers humanity. Yet the Lord gave people control of His earth and all in it. David expresses awe at the power and mercy of the God who created him.

• Should people be important to God? Why or why not? What does the fact that they are tell us about God? About ourselves?

• When you look at a starry sky, do you wonder at God's creation? How does it make you feel to be part of such a universe? What is your place in it? Have you shared David's awe of the Creator?

Psalm 11

Despite the attacks of enemies, David will not hide in a mountain stronghold; his defense is His Lord. In these verses, whether he describes a military or spiritual enemy, the king's hope lies in God.

Though others claim the world is falling apart, the psalmist continues to trust in God, who still sees everything that happens. His children, who believe in Him, may face trials, but God loves them. The wicked receive His hatred and punishment. Ultimately God's justice will prevail. Because He is faithful to His people, He will save them, while the wicked are destroyed.

• What could David trust in that would be better than God? What could be greater and more powerful than He? Even if the world were falling apart, what could he trust in?

- Is trust in a powerful Lord better than despair and doubt? If God does not immediately give you an answer to a problem, does it mean He will not answer?

WEEK TWO

Introduction

People of faith cannot simply do as they please. The call of God to faithful Christians impacts their whole lives. Those called to faith in Christ desire to serve Him with everything they have.

The psalms for this week cover a number of topics, from discouragement to thanksgiving and praise. All are part of a faith walk. God does not expect us to live Pollyanna-type lives, never facing a problem. But He does tell us that no matter what comes into our lives, He will never leave nor forsake us (Deuteronomy 31:6; Hebrews 13:5). Praise and thanks arise not from our situations, but from our appreciation of the God who supports us through them.

Some of these psalms reflect a spiritually dry period in the psalmist's life. While faith can be an exciting way to live, it does not provide continual thrills. At times, the believer may feel God becomes more distant —though God has not changed position. It may be that sin has parted the believer and God. Or it may be a time of testing, when faith is stretched and exercised, only to be made more secure in the end.

Times of testing were common in David's life as he fought for his kingdom, lost it for a while, then regained it. The struggles to fend off foreign attackers or the internal attacks of temptation further developed the king's faith. His was not a lethargic belief, but a daily struggle to come closer to God.

But David was not perfect. His only claim to faultlessness is the reflection of God's holiness in his life. As the psalmist drew near God in faith, he could increasingly live in a way that pleased Him.

Though David ultimately took part in some highly damaging sin, his heart always sought after God and felt pain when they seemed parted. He wanted to obey God, even when he failed miserably. Though his obedience is far from perfect, David wants to live for his Redeemer.

None of David's faults were hidden from God, just as none of ours can be. The faithful walk consists of a continual, habitual relationship with God, in which we confess our sins and faults to Him, ask His forgiveness, and seek to walk again in His way.

No one knew this pattern better than David. Though he fell, he always returned to God. And his legacy to us, in the psalms, is a picture of faith that has faced much and, though it has struggled, has ultimately been victorious.

The Psalms give us an intimate look at many facets of faith, from struggle to complete peace. They are all part of a consistent faith walk with Jesus.

Psalm 12

1 Help, Lord; for the godly man ceaseth; for the faithful fail from among the children of men.

2 They speak vanity every one with his neighbour: with flattering lips and with a double heart do they speak.

3 The Lord shall cut off all flattering lips, and the tongue that speaketh proud things:

4 Who have said, With our tongue will we prevail; our lips are our own: who is lord over us?

5 For the oppression of the poor, for the sighing of the needy, now will I arise, saith the Lord; I will set him in safety from him that puffeth at him.

6 The words of the Lord are pure words: as silver tried in a furnace of earth, purified seven times.

7 Thou shalt keep them, O Lord, thou shalt preserve them from this generation for ever.

8 The wicked walk on every side, when the vilest men are exalted.

Psalm 13

1 How long wilt thou forget me, O Lord? for ever? how long wilt thou hide thy face from me?

2 How long shall I take counsel in my soul, having sorrow in my heart daily? how long shall mine enemy be exalted over me?

3 Consider and hear me, O Lord my God: lighten mine eyes, lest I sleep the sleep of death;

4 Lest mine enemy say, I have prevailed against him; and those that trouble me rejoice when I am moved.

5 But I have trusted in thy mercy; my heart shall rejoice in thy salvation.

6 I will sing unto the Lord, because he hath dealt bountifully with me.

For Your Information

"Cut off": end.

"Double heart": deception.

"Take counsel in my soul": meditate, ponder.

"Lighten mine eyes": give me hope.

"Sleep the sleep of death": die.

Psalm 12

When even God's people seem to fail in faith, discouragement follows for David. How believers speak is important, because they influence others, and the psalmist obviously feels tired of being discouraged by the unbelieving words of self-reliant people. So he calls out to God, who will punish those who speak wrongly.

In comparison to those worthless human words, God responds with a valuable reassurance that encourages and blesses the psalmist—who then returns to praise as the psalm ends.

• Have the words or actions of people who claim to be Christians discouraged you? What did you conclude? How can you avoid this mistake in your own life?

• When people fail you, have you turned to God? How did that help?

Psalm 13

Like the rest of us, David had dry spiritual times when God seemed almost to have forgotten him. Here he grieves over the separation, even to the point of fearing death and the dishonor that would bring with his enemies.

As David prays his heart turns again to trust in God and His salvation. David again praises his Lord.

• Can God forget you? Is He like people in that? Why or why not?

• Have you had a time when God seemed distant? Was He really? What happened?

Psalm 14

1 The fool hath said in his heart, There is no God. They are corrupt, they have done abominable works, there is none that doeth good.

2 The Lord looked down from heaven upon the children of men, to see if there were any that did understand, and seek God.

3 They are all gone aside, they are all together become filthy: there is none that doeth good, no, not one.

4 Have all the workers of iniquity no knowledge? who eat up my people as they eat bread, and call not upon the Lord.

5 There were they in great fear: for God is in the generation of the righteous.

6 Ye have shamed the counsel of the poor, because the Lord is his refuge.

7 Oh that the salvation of Israel were come out of Zion! when the Lord bringeth back the captivity of his people, Jacob shall rejoice, and Israel shall be glad.

Psalm 15

1 Lord, who shall abide in thy tabernacle? who shall dwell in thy holy hill?

2 He that walketh uprightly, and worketh righteousness, and speaketh the truth in his heart.

3 He that backbiteth not with his tongue, nor doeth evil to his neighbour, nor taketh up a reproach against his neighbour.

4 In whose eyes a vile person is contemned; but he honoureth them that fear the Lord. He that sweareth to his own hurt, and changeth not.

5 He that putteth not out his money to usury, nor taketh reward against the innocent. He that doeth these things shall never be moved.

For Your Information

"Fool": Scripture frequently comments on the foolishness of not believing in God (see Psalm 14:1; Proverbs 1:7).

"Workers of iniquity": Wrongdoers.

"Generation of the righteous": those faithful to God.

"Jacob": another name for the man Israel, who fought with God (Genesis 32:28)—by extension, God's people.

"Tabernacle": the first place of Hebrew worship, in a tent.

"Walk uprightly": live a moral life.

"Taketh up a reproach": wrongs.

"Sweareth to his own hurt": keeps an oath, even if it hurts him.

"Usury": lending money at an exorbitant interest rate.

Psalm 14

Again, David laments the works of the wicked. But unlike many of us, he does not fear evil will ultimately win out. Even so, he wonders if anyone seeks God and is not comforted. Truly, if God's Spirit did not call us, none of us would even think of believing in Him.

Finally, David looks forward to a day when salvation will come, the people will understand God's greatness, and they will rejoice in Him.

• Have you ever thought evil might win out in the end? How did it make you feel? Where did you find hope?

• Do David's words describe your lifestyle? Why or why not? If you need to change, how can you do that?

Psalm 15

The previous psalm lamenting the works of the wicked is followed by one describing a holy lifestyle. Holiness is not simply a matter of belief. It influences actions, too, as David describes in this psalm.

• Describe how an upright person acts. How does one speaking truth in the heart act?

• From this psalm, how can you identify a holy life? A sinful one? What benefit comes to the holy person?

Psalm 16

1 Preserve me, O God: for in thee do I put my trust.

2 O my soul, thou hast said unto the Lord, Thou art my Lord: my goodness extendeth not to thee;

3 But to the saints that are in the earth, and to the excellent, in whom is all my delight.

4 Their sorrows shall be multiplied that hasten after another god: their drink offerings of blood will I not offer, nor take up their names into my lips.

5 The Lord is the portion of mine inheritance and of my cup: thou maintainest my lot.

6 The lines are fallen unto me in pleasant places; yea, I have a goodly heritage.

7 I will bless the Lord, who hath given me counsel: my reins also instruct me in the night seasons.

8 I have set the Lord always before me: because he is at my right hand, I shall not be moved.

9 Therefore my heart is glad, and my glory rejoiceth: my flesh also shall rest in hope.

10 For thou wilt not leave my soul in hell; neither wilt thou suffer thine Holy One to see corruption.

11 Thou wilt shew me the path of life: in thy presence is fulness of joy; at thy right hand there are pleasures for evermore.

Psalm 26

1 Judge me, O Lord; for I have walked in mine integrity: I have trusted also in the Lord; therefore I shall not slide.

2 Examine me, O Lord, and prove me; try my reins and my heart.

3 For thy lovingkindness is before mine eyes: and I have walked in thy truth.

4 I have not sat with vain persons, neither will I go in with dissemblers.

5 I have hated the congregation of evil doers; and will not sit with the wicked.

6 I will wash mine hands in innocency: so will I compass thine altar, O Lord:

7 That I may publish with the voice of thanksgiving, and tell of all thy wondrous works.

8 Lord, I have loved the habitation of thy house, and the place where thine honour dwelleth.

9 Gather not my soul with sinners, nor my life with bloody men:

10 In whose hands is mischief, and their right hand is full of bribes.

11 But as for me, I will walk in mine integrity: redeem me, and be merciful unto me.

12 My foot standeth in an even place: in the congregations will I bless the Lord.

For Your Information

"My goodness extendeth not to thee": I have nothing good apart from You.

"Saints": literally, "holy ones," those who trust in God.

"Drink offerings": libations.

"Lines": property boundary lines.

"Reins": center of thought and emotion.

"Right hand": a position that symbolizes God's protection or a place of power.

"Suffer": appoint.

"Walked": a consistent lifestyle following God's way.

"Holy One": More than a reference to the saints, this is a prophetic reference to Jesus and His Resurrection.

"Dissemblers": hypocrites.

"Thy house": the Temple, the Jewish place of worship.

"Bloody men": those who thirst for blood.

Psalm 16

This psalm of trust in God begins with a request by David that God will keep him safe. He describes his trust in God and delight in those who share his faith. Promising to avoid the practices of the pagan nations, he describes God as his only inheritance. The king has not been disappointed with God's gifts, both of the Promised Land and and His guidance.

Standing in a strong place, David cannot be moved from it, because he trusts in God. He rejoices in His Savior, for the life he will receive lasts not only on earth but for eternity.

• When God gives, He may give very generously. Have you received the gift of trust in the Savior? If so, have you been disappointed?

• Do you delight in God and His people? How do you know it? Do you need to spend more time with either?

Psalm 26

David opens his heart to God in this psalm, asking Him to look at his actions as he seeks to live a holy life. Though he speaks of holiness, David does not claim absolute perfection. Instead he describes his efforts to live a pure life. Finally he promises to publicly praise God, his Redeemer.

• What does it mean to walk in integrity? Is this a hallmark of your life? If not, why not? What can you do about it?

• How has David lived, in his desire to obey God? Name the specific areas he mentions in this psalm. What steps could you take to put these in your life or improve your obedience?

Psalm 17

1 Hear the right, O Lord, attend unto my cry, give ear unto my prayer, that goeth not out of feigned lips.

2 Let my sentence come forth from thy presence; let thine eyes behold the things that are equal.

3 Thou hast proved mine heart; thou hast visited me in the night; thou hast tried me, and shalt find nothing; I am purposed that my mouth shall not transgress.

4 Concerning the works of men, by the word of thy lips I have kept me from the paths of the destroyer.

5 Hold up my goings in thy paths, that my footsteps slip not.

6 I have called upon thee, for thou wilt hear me, O God: incline thine ear unto me, and hear my speech.

7 Shew thy marvellous lovingkindness, O thou that savest by thy right hand them which put their trust in thee from those that rise up against them.

8 Keep me as the apple of the eye, hide me under the shadow of thy wings,

9 From the wicked that oppress me, from my deadly enemies, who compass me about.

10 They are inclosed in their own fat: with their mouth they speak proudly.

11 They have now compassed us in our steps: they have set their eyes bowing down to the earth;

12 Like as a lion that is greedy of his prey, and as it were a young lion lurking in secret places.

13 Arise, O Lord, disappoint him, cast him down: deliver my soul from the wicked, which is thy sword:

14 From men which are thy hand, O Lord, from men of the world, which have their portion in this life, and whose belly thou fillest with thy hid treasure: they are full of children, and leave the rest of their substance to their babes.

15 As for me, I will behold thy face in righteousness: I shall be satisfied, when I awake, with thy likeness.

For Your Information

"Feigned": deceitful or hypocritical.

"Transgress": err.

"Works of men": their sinful deeds.

"Incline thine ear": listen.

"Right hand": this symbolizes power.

"Apple of the eye": something precious, to be protected.

"Shadow of thy wings": a place of protection.

"Inclosed in their own fat": closed off from God by their own prosperous greed.

Psalm 17

In this prayer for justice, probably written during Saul's attacks against David, the psalmist asks God to hear his honest prayer and judge between him and his enemy. The king uses legal language to describe his appeal to God in verse 2—he is serious about God's judgment of his "case."

David has confidence in God's ruling because has already opened his heart to his Lord, who has searched his inmost thoughts. God knows he does not want to fall into sin and that David looks to Him, not his own abilities, for protection. Verses 5–9 describe the defense the psalmist needs. Verse 10 begins a section, lasting through verse 12, that outlines the wrongdoing of David's proud and wicked enemies, who attack like wild lions.

The psalmist looks to God for refuge, knowing that even though his enemies enjoy high living today, it will not last. Even if David did not gain the throne, the joy of His righteousness through eternity would be victory enough.

• David trusts God implicitly when he asks for judgment. What characteristics of God that he mentions allowed the psalmist to do that, even though he was not perfect? Do you trust in the same descriptions of God's nature in scripture?

• What did David ask God to do for him? Have you needed such help from God? Has he provided it? How?

Psalm 18

1 I will love thee, O Lord, my strength.

2 The Lord is my rock, and my fortress, and my deliverer; my God. . .in whom I will trust. . . .

3 I will call upon the Lord. . .so shall I be saved from mine enemies.

4 The sorrows of death compassed me, and the floods of ungodly men made me afraid. . . .

6 In my distress I called upon the Lord. . .he heard my voice out of his temple. . . .

7 Then the earth shook and trembled; the foundations also of the hills moved and were shaken, because he was wroth. . . .

15 Then the channels of waters were seen, and the foundations of the world were discovered at thy rebuke, O Lord, at the blast of the breath of thy nostrils.

16 He sent from above, he took me, he drew me out of many waters.

17 He delivered me from my strong enemy. . . .

20 The Lord rewarded me according to my righteousness. . . .

21 For I have kept the ways of the Lord. . . .

22 For all his judgments were before me, and I did not put away his statutes from me. . . .

24 Therefore hath the Lord recompensed me according to my righteousness. . . .

25 With the merciful thou wilt shew thyself merciful; with an upright man. . .upright. . . .

27 For thou wilt save the afflicted people; but wilt bring down high looks.

28 For thou wilt light my candle: the Lord my God will enlighten my darkness.

29 For by thee I have run through a troop; and by my God have I leaped over a wall.

30 As for God, his way is perfect. . .he is a buckler to all those that trust in him.

31 For who is God save the Lord? or who is a rock save our God?

32 It is God that girdeth me with strength, and maketh my way perfect. . . .

35 Thou hast also given me the shield of thy salvation: and thy right hand hath holden me up, and thy gentleness hath made me great. . . .

37 I have pursued mine enemies, and overtaken them. . . .

38 They are fallen under my feet. . . .

41 They cried. . .even unto the Lord, but he answered them not.

42 Then did I beat them small as the dust before the wind: I did cast them out as the dirt in the streets.

43 Thou. . .hast made me the head of the heathen: a people whom I have not known shall serve me. . . .

46 The Lord liveth; and blessed be my rock; and let the God of my salvation be exalted.

47. . .God. . .avengeth me, and subdueth the people under me.

48 He delivereth me from mine enemies. . . .

49 Therefore will I give thanks unto thee, O Lord, among the heathen, and sing praises unto thy name.

50 Great deliverance giveth he to his king; and sheweth mercy to his anointed, to David, and to his seed for evermore.

For Your Information

"Rock": Scripture frequently compares God to a rock, because He is immovable, unchanging, and strong.

"Wroth": angry.

"Many waters": calamities.

"Statutes": God's law, as found in the first five books of the Bible, the Pentateuch.

"Buckler": shield.

"Seed": descendants.

Psalm 18

Sometime following the death of his enemy, Saul, David composed these words of praise and thanksgiving to God. There is no doubt, if one reads the Old Testament record, that God had a strong hand in keeping David from harm through the years he contended with Saul for the throne. It was a dangerous, ongoing fight for David, one he sometimes seemed very close to losing.

The psalm begins with David's expression of love and praise for his Deliverer (verses 1–6). Though David feared death, God came to his rescue.

Verses 7–15 personify God as a mighty warrior. In His anger at the wrongs done to His servant, He shows the whole earth His authority and justice. His rescue of David follows (verses 16–19). Alone, David had no hope against his enemies, but he has been faithful through trouble, so God rescued and rewarded him (verses 20–24) based on the faithfulness David had shown to his faithful Lord. All people who follow His way will find God beneficent, but the proud will feel His stern power (verses 25–29).

David rejoices in the power of God and the strength He gives those who serve Him (verses 30–42). The psalmist delights in God's deliverance of him and the authority He has conferred on him as king. Finally, the king responds with jubilant and public thanksgiving to his Lord for the line of rulers He has promised to establish.

• How has God been the Rock of your life? What has He rescued you from? Have you thanked Him?

Psalm 19

1 The heavens declare the glory of God; and the firmament sheweth his handywork.

2 Day unto day uttereth speech, and night unto night sheweth knowledge.

3 There is no speech nor language, where their voice is not heard.

4 Their line is gone out through all the earth, and their words to the end of the world. In them hath he set a tabernacle for the sun,

5 Which is as a bridegroom coming out of his chamber, and rejoiceth as a strong man to run a race.

6 His going forth is from the end of the heaven, and his circuit unto the ends of it: and there is nothing hid from the heat thereof.

7 The law of the Lord is perfect, converting the soul: the testimony of the Lord is sure, making wise the simple.

8 The statutes of the Lord are right, rejoicing the heart: the commandment of the Lord is pure, enlightening the eyes.

9 The fear of the Lord is clean, enduring for ever: the judgments of the Lord are true and righteous altogether.

10 More to be desired are they than gold, yea, than much fine gold: sweeter also than honey and the honeycomb.

11 Moreover by them is thy servant warned: and in keeping of them there is great reward.

12 Who can understand his errors? cleanse thou me from secret faults.

13 Keep back thy servant also from presumptuous sins; let them not have dominion over me: then shall I be upright, and I shall be innocent from the great transgression.

14 Let the words of my mouth, and the meditation of my heart, be acceptable in thy sight, O Lord, my strength, and my redeemer.

For Your Information

"Firmament": skies.

"Line": sound.

"Fear": awe, reverence.

"The simple": the childlike one.

"Ordinances": laws.

"Sweeter than honey": God's Word is referred to as sweet here and elsewhere (Psalm 119:103). Evil is compared to bitterness (Jeremiah 2:19; Amos 5:7; Romans 3:13).

"Thy servant": David.

Psalm 19

God's creation, the heavens, tell forth His truths in this psalm. David is not looking to the stars to tell his future. Created by God, instead this amazing sight in the skies shows forth His power throughout the earth.

Instead of looking to the skies to find truth, David looks to the scriptures. God's perfect Word reveals Him even more clearly than His creation, providing revival for the soul, guiding life choices, and offering joy. David delights in them, because they offer precious truths.

Looking at the scriptures, David becomes aware of his own hidden failings. So he seeks God's help in bypassing sin. Relying on God alone can make the heart and mind pure.

• Have you gloried in a night sky and felt the wonder of God as you did? What did it tell you about God? How are the lessons of the night sky like scripture? How do they fall short? What does this tell you about God's creation?

• When you think about God's greatness, are you humbled? Would your words and meditations please God? How could they please Him more?

Psalm 20

1 The Lord hear thee in the day of trouble; the name of the God of Jacob defend thee;

2 Send thee help from the sanctuary, and strengthen thee out of Zion;

3 Remember all thy offerings, and accept thy burnt sacrifice; Selah.

4 Grant thee according to thine own heart, and fulfil all thy counsel.

5 We will rejoice in thy salvation, and in the name of our God we will set up our banners: the Lord fulfil all thy petitions.

6 Now know I that the Lord saveth his anointed; he will hear him from his holy heaven with the saving strength of his right hand.

7 Some trust in chariots, and some in horses: but we will remember the name of the Lord our God.

8 They are brought down and fallen: but we are risen, and stand upright.

9 Save, Lord: let the king hear us when we call.

Psalm 23

1 The Lord is my shepherd; I shall not want.

2 He maketh me to lie down in green pastures: he leadeth me beside the still waters.

3 He restoreth my soul: he leadeth me in the paths of righteousness for his name's sake.

4 Yea, though I walk through the valley of the shadow of death, I will fear no evil: for thou art with me; thy rod and thy staff they comfort me.

5 Thou preparest a table before me in the presence of mine enemies: thou anointest my head with oil; my cup runneth over.

6 Surely goodness and mercy shall follow me all the days of my life: and I will dwell in the house of the Lord for ever.

For Your Information

"Accept thy burnt sacrifice": Sacrifices were part of the Old Testament rituals of forgiveness. But if a person had not truly repented and was not willing to stop sinning, God would not accept the sacrifice or offer forgiveness.

"Fulfill all thy counsel": grant your plans success.

"Banners": of an army.

"Chariots. . .and horses": symbols of earthly power.

"Shepherd": God, who guards His people. Jesus is portrayed as a shepherd in the New Testament.

"Want": lack.

"Green pastures": a place of plenty.

"Quiet waters": a restful place where sheep may easily drink.

"Shadow of death": a place of danger, perhaps threatening death.

"Rod": symbolic of authority.

"Staff": shepherd's crook, symbolizing loving guidance.

"Preparest a table": When a covenant was agreed upon, it usually included a meal, symbolizing friendship between the parties.

"Oil": symbolizes gladness.

"Cup": symbolizes abundance.

Psalm 20

For much of David's reign, Israel warred with her neighbors. This psalm is a public prayer for God's help as the nation's forces went out to battle. It is linked to Psalm 21, a praise for the victorious return from battle.

The first five verses are a prayer for the army as it sets off, wishing them well.

Instead of trusting in their armaments, the warriors express their trust in God (verses 6–9). Whenever Israel went to war, faith in God was part of their battle plan. David, the anointed king, would have been profoundly aware of God's power in battle, during Israel's history.

The warriors end with a prayer to God, asking for His salvation.

• Where are you putting your trust, when you face danger? How can God help you?

Psalm 23

Probably the best-known part of the psalter, the "shepherd's psalm" reflects David's peace with God and the early years he spend looking after sheep. But it also portrays the God who cares intimately for His people and pours out blessings on them.

This peaceful psalm describes God as a shepherd who watches over His people. He gives them the rest they need and directs their paths, just as a shepherd guides his animals, keeping them from harm. In God, we need have no fear, even when we face death, for He cares for us in all situations, and friendship with Him cannot be threatened in this world. His abundant blessings are offered to those who trust in Him.

• Do you have this kind of peace with God? If not, why not? Remember that David, who wrote the psalm, did not have a calm, peaceful life. What kind of rest is he talking about here?

• Where did David get such peace? Can you have it too?

WEEK THREE

Introduction

Certain themes and types of psalms reappear over and over in the 150 chapters of this book. David often gives God praise and thanksgiving for His help, and he frequently asks for protection from enemies. Many ideas and words used in this week's psalms should seem familiar, because David's faith firmly held on to the truths he knew about God; they became part of his regular faith walk, and he shares them with us in many of his praises and prayers.

David habitually called out to God when he faced trouble. This is why the psalms include so many prayers that ask for help against his enemies. David's battles with Saul lasted for a long time, so they are reflected often in his spiritual life. The fact that more than one psalm asks for God's aid does not mean the king did not trust Him. We all have certain ongoing needs in our lives, and these tend to reappear regularly in our prayers. God does not tell us to pray once, then never to bother Him again with that need. He wants us to continually bring our cares to Him (1 Peter 5:7). As we do, we continue to grow in faith.

We all have enemies of one sort or another. Though we may not face those who want to take our lives, either in battle or on the streets, we encounter many who disagree with our faith and cause us problems because of it. All of us daily face God's enemy, Satan, who tempts us to sin. No matter who the enemy, the principles David offers us lift up our faith as we learn to trust in God during all trials. Even if we never join the military, we can be deeply blessed by David's shared experience.

Because David shared his woes with God, the psalms have brought great comfort to suffering Christians. When we pass through trials, it's greatly encouraging to know someone else, whom God loved deeply, has been there before us and found Him faithful. In the depths of trials, many believers have turned to this book of the Bible and found comfort and direction in the midst of pain. God allowed David to share his life and faith with us. For centuries, believers have been glad he did.

Psalm 21

1 The king shall joy in thy strength, O Lord; and in thy salvation how greatly shall he rejoice!

2 Thou hast given him his heart's desire, and hast not withholden the request of his lips. Selah.

3 For thou preventest him with the blessings of goodness: thou settest a crown of pure gold on his head.

4 He asked life of thee, and thou gavest it him, even length of days for ever and ever.

His glory is great in thy salvation: honour and majesty hast thou laid upon him.

6 For thou hast made him most blessed for ever: thou hast made him exceeding glad with thy countenance.

7 For the king trusteth in the Lord, and through the mercy of the most High he shall not be moved.

8 Thine hand shall find out all thine enemies: thy right hand shall find out those that hate thee.

9 Thou shalt make them as a fiery oven in the time of thine anger: the Lord shall swallow them up in his wrath, and the fire shall devour them.

10 Their fruit shalt thou destroy from the earth, and their seed from among the children of men.

11 For they intended evil against thee: they imagined a mischievous device, which they are not able to perform.

12 Therefore shalt thou make them turn their back, when thou shalt make ready thine arrows upon thy strings against the face of them.

13 Be thou exalted, Lord, in thine own strength: so will we sing and praise thy power.

Psalm 24

1 The earth is the Lord's, and the fulness thereof; the world, and they that dwell therein.

2 For he hath founded it upon the seas, and established it upon the floods.

3 Who shall ascend into the hill of the Lord? or who shall stand in his holy place?

4 He that hath clean hands, and a pure heart; who hath not lifted up his soul unto vanity, nor sworn deceitfully.

5 He shall receive the blessing from the Lord, and righteousness from the God of his salvation.

6 This is the generation of them that seek him, that seek thy face, O Jacob. Selah.

7 Lift up your heads, O ye gates; and be ye lift up, ye everlasting doors; and the King of glory shall come in.

8 Who is this King of glory? The Lord strong and mighty, the Lord mighty in battle.

9 Lift up your heads, O ye gates; even lift them up, ye everlasting doors; and the King of glory shall come in.

10 Who is this King of glory? The Lord of hosts, he is the King of glory. Selah.

For Your Information

"Joy": rejoice.

"Mischievous device": evil plot.

"Countenance": face. Seeing God's face means to be in His presence.

"Fullness thereof": all that fills it.

"Hill of the Lord": Jerusalem's temple.

"Generation": type of people.

"Gates": either of the city or temple.

Psalm 21

This and Psalm 20 are complementary psalms. Some commentators also see them as Messianic psalms, praising the Redeemer.

Here, the king and the people praise God, who preserved their king and led him to conquest. God's strength turned back an enemy that hated both Israel and God. In scripture, an attack on Israel is also often seen as an attack upon their Lord. So God made the enemy a target for his wrath and destroyed them.

- How is God your King? What kind of praise does He deserve from you?

- Has God led you to victories? Have you thanked and praised Him for His faithfulness? Is that attitude a part of your regular Christian walk?

Psalm 24

This worship psalm was written either when David brought of the ark of the covenant to Jerusalem (2 Samuel 6) or a festival remembering that event. The ark, Israel's most holy object, used on the Day of Atonement to picture forgiveness of sin, contained the Ten Commandments' tablets, a jar of manna, and Aaron's rod.

The psalmist begins with praise for the Creator (verses 1–2). Then the sanctified person who can approach God is described in detail (verses 3–6). Praise for God, the King of Glory (verses 7–10), ends the psalm.

- Does the thought that God has forgiven your sins make you want to praise Him? If not, is it because sin has overtaken your life, and you need to ask for forgiveness?

Psalm 22

1 My God, my God, why hast thou forsaken me? why art thou so far from helping me, and from the words of my roaring?

2 O my God, I cry in the daytime, but thou hearest not; and in the night season, and am not silent.

3 But thou art holy, O thou that inhabitest the praises of Israel.

4 Our fathers trusted in thee: they trusted, and thou didst deliver them.

5 They cried unto thee, and were delivered: they trusted in thee, and were not confounded.

6 But I am a worm, and no man; a reproach of men, and despised of the people.

7 All they that see me laugh me to scorn: they shoot out the lip, they shake the head, saying,

8 He trusted on the Lord that he would deliver him: let him deliver him, seeing he delighted in him.

9 But thou art he that took me out of the womb: thou didst make me hope when I was upon my mother's breasts.

10 I was cast upon thee from the womb: thou art my God from my mother's belly.

11 Be not far from me; for trouble is near; for there is none to help.

12 Many bulls have compassed me: strong bulls of Bashan have beset me round.

13 They gaped upon me with their mouths, as a ravening and a roaring lion.

14 I am poured out like water, and all my bones are out of joint: my heart is like wax; it is melted in the midst of my bowels.

15 My strength is dried up like a potsherd; and my tongue cleaveth to my jaws; and thou hast brought me into the dust of death.

16 For dogs have compassed me: the assembly of the wicked have inclosed me: they pierced my hands and my feet.

17 I may tell all my bones: they look and stare upon me.

18 They part my garments among them, and cast lots upon my vesture.

19 But be not thou far from me, O Lord: O my strength, haste thee to help me.

20 Deliver my soul from the sword; my darling from the power of the dog.

21 Save me from the lion's mouth: for thou hast heard me from the horns of the unicorns.

22 I will declare thy name unto my brethren: in the midst of the congregation will I praise thee.

23 Ye that fear the Lord, praise him; all ye the seed of Jacob, glorify him; and fear him, all ye the seed of Israel.

24 For he hath not despised nor abhorred the affliction of the afflicted; neither hath he hid his face from him; but when he cried unto him, he heard.

25 My praise shall be of thee in the great congregation: I will pay my vows before them that fear him.

26 The meek shall eat and be satisfied: they shall praise the Lord that seek him: your heart shall live for ever.

27 All the ends of the world shall remember and turn unto the Lord: and all the kindreds of the nations shall worship before thee.

28 For the kingdom is the Lord's: and he is the governor among the nations.

29 All they that be fat upon earth shall eat and worship: all they that go down to the dust shall bow before him: and none can keep alive his own soul.

30 A seed shall serve him; it shall be accounted to the Lord for a generation.

31 They shall come, and shall declare his righteousness unto a people that shall be born, that he hath done this.

For Your Information

"Roaring": noises made in misery.

"Season": time.

"Hope": in God.

"Heart": in this case, a reference to the spirit. With the earlier reference to bones in this verse, which imply the body, this is speaking of the whole person.

"Potsherd": broken piece of pottery.

"Cleaveth": sticks.

"Dogs": a feral pack of dogs.

"Vesture": clothing.

"Unicorns": better translated buffalo.

"Hid his face": a sign of God's disfavor.

Psalm 22

Hundreds of years before the Crucifixion, David wrote this psalm that clearly prophesies the sufferings of Jesus on the Cross. Jesus quoted its first verse while He was there (Matthew 27:46).

Verses 6–8 describe the mocking Jesus received on the Cross. Matthew 27:39, 43 clearly describe these prophecies being fulfilled.

Verses 12–18 describe Jesus' physical suffering and events during the crucifixion. His enemies mocked him (Matthew 27:39–44). Crucifixion would have disjointed his bones and pierced his hands and feet. Matthew 27:35 describes the division of His clothing by the soldiers who did the deed.

Parts of the psalm also apply to the suffering believer, who does not understand what is happening and seeks the relief of God's justice. Many Christians have found comfort in these words, as they have sought to understand their pain. Though they probably haven't experienced crucifixion, they can relate to suffering that makes one intensely vulnerable.

The only response the believer can offer in suffering is trust that God will deliver (verses 19–21). When that happens, praise in public will share the news of God's faithfulness and lead to praise among the faithful. Even those who are yet to live will share in the joy of God's faithfulness.

- Whom do you turn to when you face suffering? Are you tempted to blame God or seek His help? Which choice will bring you more benefit?

- When God has been faithful and ended your suffering, have you praised Him publicly?

Psalm 25

1 Unto thee, O Lord, do I lift up my soul.

2 O my God, I trust in thee: let me not be ashamed, let not mine enemies triumph over me.

3 Yea, let none that wait on thee be ashamed: let them be ashamed which transgress without cause.

4 Shew me thy ways, O Lord; teach me thy paths.

5 Lead me in thy truth, and teach me: for thou art the God of my salvation; on thee do I wait all the day.

6 Remember, O Lord, thy tender mercies and thy lovingkindnesses; for they have been ever of old.

7 Remember not the sins of my youth, nor my transgressions: according to thy mercy remember thou me for thy goodness' sake, O Lord.

8 Good and upright is the Lord: therefore will he teach sinners in the way.

9 The meek will he guide in judgment: and the meek will he teach his way.

10 All the paths of the Lord are mercy and truth unto such as keep his covenant and his testimonies.

11 For thy name's sake, O Lord, pardon mine iniquity; for it is great.

12 What man is he that feareth the Lord? him shall he teach in the way that he shall choose.

13 His soul shall dwell at ease; and his seed shall inherit the earth.

14 The secret of the Lord is with them that fear him; and he will shew them his covenant.

15 Mine eyes are ever toward the Lord; for he shall pluck my feet out of the net.

16 Turn thee unto me, and have mercy upon me; for I am desolate and afflicted.

17 The troubles of my heart are enlarged: O bring thou me out of my distresses.

18 Look upon mine affliction and my pain; and forgive all my sins.

19 Consider mine enemies; for they are many; and they hate me with cruel hatred.

20 O keep my soul, and deliver me: let me not be ashamed; for I put my trust in thee.

21 Let integrity and uprightness preserve me; for I wait on thee.
22 Redeem Israel, O God, out of all his troubles.

For Your Information

"Ashamed": put to shame, disappointed.

"Guide in judgment": show the right way.

"Covenant": a formal agreement between two individuals or groups that define their relationship. God made an agreement with His people, defining the blessings He would offer if they would follow Him.

"Inherit the earth": receive both earthly and spiritual blessings from God.

"Net": a trap of the enemy.

Psalm 25

Though we don't know just when David wrote this, it is not one of his earlier psalms, since he refers to his past youth (verse 7). He seems clearly aware of how far his life has fallen short of God's holiness and how much he needs divine help. The sin he would like to eradicate from his life impinges on his life again.

First, the psalmist declares his trust in God and need for salvation from his enemies. Humbly, he asks God to show him His paths, be merciful, and not hold his youthful sins against him. God's way, and His assistance in walking in it, are the solutions to the sin problem David faces.

Humbled by God's mercy even in His acknowledging of humanity, with all its flaws, the king delights in the blessings God has promised in His covenant. He seeks God's rescue from his afflictions and sins and asks for His redemption.

• Has sin impinged on your life? Like the psalmist, has it made you aware of your need for God, or has it driven you far from Him?

- How do you most often respond, when you face temptation? Do you need to change the way you respond or protect yourself before you feel tempted?

- Are you trying to walk in God's paths? What advice on that subject does David give in this psalm?

Psalm 27

1 The Lord is my light and my salvation; whom shall I fear? the Lord is the strength of my life; of whom shall I be afraid?

2 When the wicked, even mine enemies and my foes, came upon me to eat up my flesh, they stumbled and fell.

3 Though an host should encamp against me, my heart shall not fear: though war should rise against me, in this will I be confident.

4 One thing have I desired of the Lord, that will I seek after; that I may dwell in the house of the Lord all the days of my life, to behold the beauty of the Lord, and to inquire in his temple.

5 For in the time of trouble he shall hide me in his pavilion: in the secret of his tabernacle shall he hide me; he shall set me up upon a rock.

6 And now shall mine head be lifted up above mine enemies round about me: therefore will I offer in his tabernacle sacrifices of joy; I will sing, yea, I will sing praises unto the Lord.

7 Hear, O Lord, when I cry with my voice: have mercy also upon me, and answer me.

8 When thou saidst, Seek ye my face; my heart said unto thee, Thy face, Lord, will I seek.

9 Hide not thy face far from me; put not thy servant away in anger: thou hast been my help; leave me not, neither forsake me, O God of my salvation.

10 When my father and my mother forsake me, then the Lord will take me up.

11 Teach me thy way, O Lord, and lead me in a plain path, because of mine enemies.

12 Deliver me not over unto the will of mine enemies: for false witnesses are risen up against me, and such as breathe out cruelty.

13 I had fainted, unless I had believed to see the goodness of the Lord in the land of the living.

14 Wait on the Lord: be of good courage, and he shall strengthen thine heart: wait, I say, on the Lord.

For Your Information

"Light": God is often referred to as light (see, for example, Isaiah 60:1; Matthew 5:14). He guides the believer and gives understanding.

"Enquire in his temple": seek God's will in His holy tabernacle.

"Pavilion": dwelling place.

"Set me up upon a rock": put me in a place where I can stand firm. When He is spoken of as Deliverer, God is often spoken of as a rock (see Psalm 28:1).

"False witnesses": liars or those in error, but any who are not speaking what is true.

Psalm 27

In an intensely personal psalm, David speaks of God as his light, the one who lights his way, and his salvation. God is not simply an "out there" being, but the center of David's existence. He has kept David alive, when others wanted him dead. His Savior has protected the king and put him in a strong place. Because God is with him, the psalmist need not fear.

In response, David's one desire is to spend time with God. Verses 4–5 speak of this desire for intimacy with God, using descriptions of the tabernacle, where sacrifices for sin were made and the Jews drew near to God.

David has sought God in all his troubles, and God has responded faithfully. Yet the king is still aware of his continual need for God's mercy and protection. He ends with counsel that those who trust Him need to wait on God for the strength they need.

• Could you describe God as your light? What does this idea mean? How could it affect your life?

• What is the one desire of your life? Would God approve? If not, what do you need to change?

Psalm 28

1 Unto thee will I cry, O Lord my rock; be not silent to me: lest, if thou be silent to me, I become like them that go down into the pit.

2 Hear the voice of my supplications, when I cry unto thee, when I lift up my hands toward thy holy oracle.

3 Draw me not away with the wicked, and with the workers of iniquity, which speak peace to their neighbours, but mischief is in their hearts.

4 Give them according to their deeds, and according to the wickedness of their endeavours: give them after the work of their hands; render to them their desert.

5 Because they regard not the works of the Lord, nor the operation of his hands, he shall destroy them, and not build them up.

6 Blessed be the Lord, because he hath heard the voice of my supplications.

7 The Lord is my strength and my shield; my heart trusted in him, and I am helped: therefore my heart greatly rejoiceth; and with my song will I praise him.

8 The Lord is their strength, and he is the saving strength of his anointed.

9 Save thy people, and bless thine inheritance: feed them also, and lift them up for ever.

Psalm 29

1 Give unto the Lord, O ye mighty, give unto the Lord glory and strength.

2 Give unto the Lord the glory due unto his name; worship the Lord in the beauty of holiness.

3 The voice of the Lord is upon the waters: the God of glory thundereth: the Lord is upon many waters.

4 The voice of the Lord is powerful; the voice of the Lord is full of majesty.

5 The voice of the Lord breaketh the cedars; yea, the Lord breaketh the cedars of Lebanon.

6 He maketh them also to skip like a calf; Lebanon and Sirion like a young unicorn.

7 The voice of the Lord divideth the flames of fire.

8 The voice of the Lord shaketh the wilderness; the Lord shaketh the wilderness of Kadesh.

9 The voice of the Lord maketh the hinds to calve, and discovereth the forests: and in his temple doth every one speak of his glory.

10 The Lord sitteth upon the flood; yea, the Lord sitteth king for ever.

11 The Lord will give strength unto his people; the Lord will bless his people with peace.

For Your Information

"Pit": grave. If God is silent, David will be like a dead man.

"Oracle": the inner sanctuary of the tabernacle, which held the ark of the covenant.

"Their desert": what they deserve.

"Supplications": a prayer that humbly requests something from God.

"Beauty of holiness": God's holiness is beautiful, but this also may refer to the tabernacle.

"Cedars of Lebanon": large and beautiful pine trees often used for building in David's age.

Psalm 28

Again David cries out to God, praying for deliverance from his enemies and God's justice against them. He does not want to be like the evil ones, whose just deserts would be disaster.

As God hears his prayers, David rejoices with thanksgiving and prayer. Then he declares God's salvation and asks Him to save, feed, and encourage His people.

• Like David, do you constantly call out to God when you are in trouble? Do you also reach out to Him when your life seems good?

• David constantly seems aware of how easily he could fall into sin. Do you feel this way, too, or do you feel as if you could never fall? Which is the godlier attitude?

Psalm 29

In a psalm of praise, David uses pictures of His creation to describe the Creator. God's majesty speaks in the oceans and His authority covers the whole earth, breaking powerful trees, ruling over fire, and shaking the land.

David glorifies God for His power and is thankful for the blessings He gives to His people.

- God's holiness should be beautiful to His people. Is this true for you? If not, is sin impeding your ability to appreciate His holiness?

- When some natural disaster occurs, is it out of God's control? Can He help those affected by it?

Psalm 30

1 I will extol thee, O Lord; for thou hast lifted me up, and hast not made my foes to rejoice over me.

2 O Lord my God, I cried unto thee, and thou hast healed me.

3 O Lord, thou hast brought up my soul from the grave: thou hast kept me alive, that I should not go down to the pit.

4 Sing unto the Lord, O ye saints of his, and give thanks at the remembrance of his holiness.

5 For his anger endureth but a moment; in his favour is life: weeping may endure for a night, but joy cometh in the morning.

6 And in my prosperity I said, I shall never be moved.

7 Lord, by thy favour thou hast made my mountain to stand strong: thou didst hide thy face, and I was troubled.

8 I cried to thee, O Lord; and unto the Lord I made supplication.

9 What profit is there in my blood, when I go down to the pit? Shall the dust praise thee? shall it declare thy truth?

10 Hear, O Lord, and have mercy upon me: Lord, be thou my helper.

11 Thou hast turned for me my mourning into dancing: thou hast put off my sackcloth, and girded me with gladness;

12 To the end that my glory may sing praise to thee, and not be silent. O Lord my God, I will give thanks unto thee for ever.

Psalm 32

1 Blessed is he whose transgression is forgiven, whose sin is covered.

2 Blessed is the man unto whom the Lord imputeth not iniquity, and in whose spirit there is no guile.

3 When I kept silence, my bones waxed old through my roaring all the day long.

4 For day and night thy hand was heavy upon me: my moisture is turned into the drought of summer. Selah.

5 I acknowledged my sin unto thee, and mine iniquity have I not hid. I said, I will confess my transgressions unto the Lord; and thou forgavest the iniquity of my sin. Selah.

6 For this shall every one that is godly pray unto thee in a time when thou mayest be found: surely in the floods of great waters they shall not come nigh unto him.

7 Thou art my hiding place; thou shalt preserve me from trouble; thou shalt compass me about with songs of deliverance. Selah.

8 I will instruct thee and teach thee in the way which thou shalt go: I will guide thee with mine eye.

9 Be ye not as the horse, or as the mule, which have no understanding: whose mouth must be held in with bit and bridle, lest they come near unto thee.

10 Many sorrows shall be to the wicked: but he that trusteth in the Lord, mercy shall compass him about.

11 Be glad in the Lord, and rejoice, ye righteous: and shout for joy, all ye that are upright in heart.

For Your Information

"Healed me": The psalmist has been healed of affliction, as of a disease.

"Anger": God's anger is always a holy anger at sin. Though it may last a short while, His forgiveness is eternal.

"Hide thy face:" a personification of God, indicating that the psalmist feels distant from Him.

"Sackcloth": a rough cloth, worn to indicate penitence.

"Covered": a picture of the blood that covers over sin. This was the purpose of Old Testament sacrifices. Jesus' sacrifice on the cross was the final covering for sin.

"Waxed": became.

"Imputeth": made a legal charge.

"Moisture": bodily fluids.

"Floods of great waters": the phrase indicates dangers.

"Hiding place": a place of safety.

Psalm 30

The superscription for this psalm reads "at the dedication of the house of David." Commentators connect this with the completed building of

David's house (2 Samuel 5:11), the rededication of David's house after Absalom violated his father's concubines (2 Samuel 16:21–22), or the dedication of materials for the temple (1 Chronicles 29:1–9). Though David wanted to build the temple, God denied him that right, because he was a man of war (1 Chronicles 28:3), so instead David made preparations for its being built by his son, Solomon.

The psalmist rejoices in God's favor and answers to prayers for help. He calls on all believers to praise His holiness. Though David faced troubles and doubts, God was faithful, and he rejoices and praises God.

- Have you feared that God would not come to your aid in trouble? Did He?

Psalm 32

David rejoices in forgiven sin (verses 1–2), and tells of the agonies of his own determined sinning (verses 3–4). He calls on all believers to follow his example and pray, so they may receive instruction from God and be controlled and blessed by Him.

The psalm ends with a call for all to praise God.

- Has God forgiven your sin? How do you know? (Read John 3:16; Romans 10:13; John 1:8–10).

- Have you felt the pain of determined sin? The joy of sin forgiven? Did forgiveness cause you to praise God?

Psalm 31

1 In thee, O Lord, do I put my trust; let me never be ashamed: deliver me in thy righteousness.

2 Bow down thine ear to me; deliver me speedily: be thou my strong rock. . . .

3 For thou art my rock and my fortress; therefore for thy name's sake lead me, and guide me.

4 Pull me out of the net that they have laid privily for me: for thou art my strength.

5 Into thine hand I commit my spirit: thou hast redeemed me, O Lord God of truth.

6 I have hated them that regard lying vanities: but I trust in the Lord.

7 I will be glad and rejoice in thy mercy: for thou hast considered my trouble; thou hast known my soul in adversities;

8 And hast not shut me up into the hand of the enemy: thou hast set my feet in a large room.

9 Have mercy upon me, O Lord, for I am in trouble: mine eye is consumed with grief. . . .

10 For my life is spent with grief, and my years with sighing: my strength faileth because of mine iniquity. . . .

11 I was a reproach among all mine enemies, but especially among my neighbours, and a fear to mine acquaintance: they that did see me without fled from me.

12 I am forgotten as a dead man out of mind: I am like a broken vessel.

13 For I have heard the slander of many: fear was on every side: while they took counsel together against me, they devised to take away my life.

14 But I trusted in thee, O Lord: I said, Thou art my God.

15 My times are in thy hand: deliver me from the hand of mine enemies. . . .

16 Make thy face to shine upon thy servant: save me for thy mercies' sake.

17 Let me not be ashamed, O Lord; for I have called upon thee: let the wicked be ashamed, and let them be silent in the grave.

18 Let the lying lips be put to silence; which speak grievous things proudly and contemptuously against the righteous.

19 Oh how great is thy goodness, which thou hast laid up for them that fear thee; which thou hast wrought for them that trust in thee before the sons of men!

20 Thou shalt hide them in the secret of thy presence from the pride of man: thou shalt keep them secretly in a pavilion from the strife of tongues.

21 Blessed be the Lord: for he hath shewed me his marvellous kindness in a strong city.

22 For I said in my haste, I am cut off from before thine eyes: nevertheless thou heardest the voice of my supplications when I cried unto thee.

23 O love the Lord, all ye his saints: for the Lord preserveth the faithful, and plentifully rewardeth the proud doer.

24 Be of good courage, and he shall strengthen your heart, all ye that hope in the Lord.

For Your Information

"Commit my spirit": The trusting psalmist commits his life to God.

"Redeemed": Those who believe in Him are bought back from sin by God (Psalm 34:22; Romans 3:23–24). This is a repeated Old and New Testament theme. In the Old Testament it prefigures forgiveness of sin through the sacrifice of Jesus.

"Spent": wasted.

"Consumed": decayed.

"In a large room": in a place of much freedom. He is not confined by enemies.

"Thy face to shine": an expression of God's favor.

"Strong city": a besieged city.

Psalm 31

This psalm of trust and prayer for God's continued deliverance and protection continues David's appreciation of God's perpetual care. But it also expresses his grief over the continuing attacks by friends who are now enemies.

In the first eight verses, David declares his own trust in God and his need for help. He places himself in God's hands entirely, and hates those who do not love Him. Verses 9–18 describe David's troubles in detail, including his desertion by his friends and their slander against him. In all this, he remained faithful.

Finally, David reminds himself and his readers of God's goodness and salvation and calls everyone to love and hope in Him.

• Faith grows when it is tested by trials. Have you ever been tested? Did your faith grow?

• Trust is not a one-time thing. Have you faced a trial more than once? Did that mean God did not know of your struggle or did not care? What would David tell you?

WEEK FOUR

Introduction

This week, we cover a range of psalms. King David experienced God in many situations, and his works reflect his life. Often his praise for God becomes excited and exuberant. Psalm 33 ecstatically calls all Israel to remember the power of the God whom they serve. The king reminds his people the Lord is always in control, no matter what the country experiences. In the next psalm, David considers the happiness God offers believers and praises Him for it. Contrary to the beliefs of those who do not know Him, loving God is a joyful experience, and David's praise psalms show it.

But the wicked are always with us, as Psalm 36 comments, and the faithful need God's protection against them. However, their evil deeds cannot overwhelm divine love. From the anguish of watching evil, David moves into the delight of praise for the One whose mercy cannot be challenged. He trusts in God, even as he faces iniquity.

Yet David is also keenly aware of the awful impact his own sin can have on his relationship with God. Frequently in this set of psalms he admits that his troubles are his own fault, for he has sinned. Psalms 38–41 take up this theme, in which the psalmist speaks of suffering in body and soul, and even death. Sin affects the whole being, and as hard as David seeks to obey, it continues to disturb his life. Though believers seek to obey God and live in His ways, sin dogs our steps until we reach heaven. But even in the midst of sorrow, David recognizes God's blessings as he calls out again and again to God his Savior.

David's failings and God's grace contrast powerfully. Though the king continually seeks to obey, fails, and fails again, God's grace never expires. He has chosen David, both as His child and as king, and that choice will not change. Despite David's doubts and fears, God always protects and supports him.

It is humbling to know how much we share David's failings, but our hope ignites when we know that God offers us, too, these immense blessings. Even when we are not faithful, He is. His grace does not leave us, once our hearts have been changed.

Psalm 33

1 Rejoice in the Lord, O ye righteous: for praise is comely for the upright.

2 Praise the Lord with harp: sing unto him with the psaltery and an instrument of ten strings.

3 Sing unto him a new song; play skilfully with a loud noise.

4 For the word of the Lord is right; and all his works are done in truth.

5 He loveth righteousness and judgment: the earth is full of the goodness of the Lord.

6 By the word of the Lord were the heavens made; and all the host of them by the breath of his mouth.

7 He gathereth the waters of the sea together as an heap: he layeth up the depth in storehouses.

8 Let all the earth fear the Lord: let all the inhabitants of the world stand in awe of him.

9 For he spake, and it was done; he commanded, and it stood fast.

10 The Lord bringeth the counsel of the heathen to nought: he maketh the devices of the people of none effect.

11 The counsel of the Lord standeth for ever, the thoughts of his heart to all generations.

12 Blessed is the nation whose God is the Lord; and the people whom he hath chosen for his own inheritance.

13 The Lord looketh from heaven; he beholdeth all the sons of men.

14 From the place of his habitation he looketh upon all the inhabitants of the earth.

15 He fashioneth their hearts alike; he considereth all their works.

16 There is no king saved by the multitude of an host: a mighty man is not delivered by much strength.

17 An horse is a vain thing for safety: neither shall he deliver any by his great strength.

18 Behold, the eye of the Lord is upon them that fear him, upon them that hope in his mercy;

19 To deliver their soul from death, and to keep them alive in famine.

20 Our soul waiteth for the Lord: he is our help and our shield.

21 For our heart shall rejoice in him, because we have trusted in his holy name.

22 Let thy mercy, O Lord, be upon us, according as we hope in thee.

For Your Information
"Comely": beautiful.

"Psaltery": an ancient instrument something like a zither.

"An instrument of ten strings": a lyre.

"Loveth": delights in doing.

"Spake": spoke.

"Nought": nothing.

"Fashioneth": creates.

"Horse": In David's age, some warriors rode into battle on horses. He speaks of a battle horse as an earthly protection, but one that is nothing compared to God. For a description of a horse in battle, read Job 39:19–25.

Psalm 33
This orphan psalm calls the faithful to praise, using many instruments and playing them with great skill. This may have been a responsive liturgy, between a priestly choir and the people.

Following the call to praise, God is worshiped for his righteousness and wonders of creation (verses 4–8). All people are encouraged to revere God, who controls the lives and thoughts of all humanity, including those who do not believe in Him. The weakness of even the strongest earthly power is compared to the Lord's strength, and His power to deliver those who trust in Him depicted. Praise and a cry for mercy end the psalm.

• Why is praise becoming to God's people? The psalmist gives us many reasons to praise God—list at least six he names here. How have they made a difference in your life?

Psalm 34

1 I will bless the Lord at all times: his praise shall continually be in my mouth.

2 My soul shall make her boast in the Lord: the humble shall hear thereof, and be glad.

3 O magnify the Lord with me, and let us exalt his name together.

4 I sought the Lord, and he heard me, and delivered me from all my fears.

5 They looked unto him, and were lightened: and their faces were not ashamed.

6 This poor man cried, and the Lord heard him, and saved him out of all his troubles.

7 The angel of the Lord encampeth round about them that fear him, and delivereth them.

8 O taste and see that the Lord is good: blessed is the man that trusteth in him.

9 O fear the Lord, ye his saints: for there is no want to them that fear him.

10 The young lions do lack, and suffer hunger: but they that seek the Lord shall not want any good thing.

11 Come, ye children, hearken unto me: I will teach you the fear of the Lord.

12 What man is he that desireth life, and loveth many days, that he may see good?

13 Keep thy tongue from evil, and thy lips from speaking guile.

14 Depart from evil, and do good; seek peace, and pursue it.

15 The eyes of the Lord are upon the righteous, and his ears are open unto their cry.

16 The face of the Lord is against them that do evil, to cut off the remembrance of them from the earth.

17 The righteous cry, and the Lord heareth, and delivereth them out of all their troubles.

18 The Lord is nigh unto them that are of a broken heart; and saveth such as be of a contrite spirit.

19 Many are the afflictions of the righteous: but the Lord delivereth him out of them all.

20 He keepeth all his bones: not one of them is broken.

21 Evil shall slay the wicked: and they that hate the righteous shall be desolate.

22 The Lord redeemeth the soul of his servants: and none of them that trust in him shall be desolate.

For Your Information

"Bless": extol.

"Magnify": glorify.

"Poor": not a person lacking in finances or goods, but one unable to save himself.

"Angel of the Lord": God's messenger.

"Encampeth round about them": a picture of protection, as in a surrounding army.

"Children": This is not only directed to children, but to all the psalmist's listeners.

"All his bones": his whole being.

Psalm 34

In the first verses of this psalm, David calls all who hear him (or read his words) to praise God exuberantly. Verses 4–7 picture some of the psalmist's reasons for praise and repeats His promise of protection.

God means us to thoroughly experience His love, as David describes in verse 8, when He compares knowing God's love to the physical senses of tasting and seeing. The following two verses promise that believers will lack nothing. In verses 11–14, David offers guidance on how to live out that kind of faith. The next four verses give examples of God's faithful response to those who have been made right with Him.

Finally, David rejoices in God's victory over sin and His salvation of those who serve Him. God is ever faithful to the faithful.

• If you were going to write a psalm, what reasons for praise would you have? What has He done in your life?

- What has God protected you from? Did you understand what He was doing at the time? If not, how did you react?

- Have you ever lacked anything? Have you ever lacked anything you really needed to live faithfully? What is the difference? Which does God provide?

- Are you doing the things David advises for a close walk with God? Where could you improve? What can you thank God for?

Psalm 36

1 The transgression of the wicked saith within my heart, that there is no fear of God before his eyes.

2 For he flattereth himself in his own eyes, until his iniquity be found to be hateful.

3 The words of his mouth are iniquity and deceit: he hath left off to be wise, and to do good.

4 He deviseth mischief upon his bed; he setteth himself in a way that is not good; he abhorreth not evil.

5 Thy mercy, O Lord, is in the heavens; and thy faithfulness reacheth unto the clouds.

6 Thy righteousness is like the great mountains; thy judgments are a great deep: O Lord, thou preservest man and beast.

7 How excellent is thy lovingkindness, O God! therefore the children of men put their trust under the shadow of thy wings.

8 They shall be abundantly satisfied with the fatness of thy house; and thou shalt make them drink of the river of thy pleasures.

9 For with thee is the fountain of life: in thy light shall we see light.

10 O continue thy lovingkindness unto them that know thee; and thy righteousness to the upright in heart.

11 Let not the foot of pride come against me, and let not the hand of the wicked remove me.

12 There are the workers of iniquity fallen: they are cast down, and shall not be able to rise.

For Your Information

"Until his iniquity be found to be hateful": His sin has found him out and he suffers from its consequences (see also Numbers 32:23).

"Fatness": abundance.

"In thy light shall we see light": God's illumination of the human spirit gives spiritual life and the ability to understand and enjoy spiritual truth.

Psalm 36

As he begins, David comments on the intense sinfulness of the wicked, in whom God inspires no awe. Because the evil man looks good in his own eyes, he cannot even imagine the destruction that awaits him as a result of his own wrongs. He becomes wholly focused on wickedness and ceases to do good.

God's deep and wide love, described in verses 5–9, contrasts starkly with the wickedness of man. To those who seek His righteousness, God makes all good things available. But only those who love Him can see these treasures He has to offer. Once we know His life, we also have light to understand His blessings.

David ends by seeking God's continued blessings for his people and asking for personal protection from the wicked. In the last line, he rejoices that evildoers have been overcome.

- Have you also been discouraged by the attitude of obviously wicked people? Is God aware of them? If He has not stopped their wickedness yet, will He? Name two ways He might deal with it.

- Has God given you His light? If so, what kind of difference has it made in your understanding?

Psalm 38

1 O Lord, rebuke me not in thy wrath: neither chasten me in thy hot displeasure.

2 For thine arrows stick fast in me, and thy hand presseth me sore.

3 There is no soundness in my flesh because of thine anger; neither is there any rest in my bones because of my sin.

4 For mine iniquities are gone over mine head: as an heavy burden they are too heavy for me.

5 My wounds stink and are corrupt because of my foolishness.

6 I am troubled; I am bowed down greatly; I go mourning all the day long.

7 For my loins are filled with a loathsome disease: and there is no soundness in my flesh.

8 I am feeble and sore broken: I have roared by reason of the disquietness of my heart.

9 Lord, all my desire is before thee; and my groaning is not hid from thee.

10 My heart panteth, my strength faileth me: as for the light of mine eyes, it also is gone from me.

11 My lovers and my friends stand aloof from my sore; and my kinsmen stand afar off.

12 They also that seek after my life lay snares for me: and they that seek my hurt speak mischievous things, and imagine deceits all the day long.

13 But I, as a deaf man, heard not; and I was as a dumb man that openeth not his mouth.

14 Thus I was as a man that heareth not, and in whose mouth are no reproofs.

15 For in thee, O Lord, do I hope: thou wilt hear, O Lord my God.

16 For I said, Hear me, lest otherwise they should rejoice over me: when my foot slippeth, they magnify themselves against me.

17 For I am ready to halt, and my sorrow is continually before me.

18 For I will declare mine iniquity; I will be sorry for my sin.

19 But mine enemies are lively, and they are strong: and they that hate me wrongfully are multiplied.

20 They also that render evil for good are mine adversaries; because I follow the thing that good is.

21 Forsake me not, O Lord: O my God, be not far from me.

22 Make haste to help me, O Lord my salvation.

For Your Information

"Arrows": a picture of how God's anger hurts the psalmist as if it were a physical pain.

"Are corrupt": fester.

Psalm 38

Here David expresses penitence and pain as he suffers under the effect of his own sin and the wrongdoing of others. The first six verses detail the weight of his own sins, though he does not specify what they were. They have brought him to continual mourning.

Not only is the psalmist's spirit broken, so is his body (verses 7–8, 10). He hurts in many places, and because of it, even those whom he loves most have deserted him. Enemies have begun causing all kinds of mischief as they delight in his troubles, but David has not responded to them. His hope lies in God, not men.

David does not hide his sin from God (who knew of it anyway). He has admitted his own wrongs, but it hurts him to see his enemies, who hate him because he does right, delighting in his downfall.

He ends by asking God not to forsake him, but to hurry to his help. As we know from David's other psalms, he does not doubt God will answer.

• Have you felt the pain of sin and the weight of guilt? What was your solution to the problem? What would David advise you to do?

• When friends and family desert you, do you still have one to help? How has God helped you when no one else would or could?

• How can you be certain God answered David? Do you have the same confidence as the psalmist that God will come to your rescue? Why or why not?

Psalm 39

1 I said, I will take heed to my ways, that I sin not with my tongue: I will keep my mouth with a bridle, while the wicked is before me.

2 I was dumb with silence, I held my peace, even from good; and my sorrow was stirred.

3 My heart was hot within me, while I was musing the fire burned: then spake I with my tongue,

4 Lord, make me to know mine end, and the measure of my days, what it is: that I may know how frail I am.

5 Behold, thou hast made my days as an handbreadth; and mine age is as nothing before thee: verily every man at his best state is altogether vanity. Selah.

6 Surely every man walketh in a vain shew: surely they are disquieted in vain: he heapeth up riches, and knoweth not who shall gather them.

7 And now, Lord, what wait I for? my hope is in thee.

8 Deliver me from all my transgressions: make me not the reproach of the foolish.

9 I was dumb, I opened not my mouth; because thou didst it.

10 Remove thy stroke away from me: I am consumed by the blow of thine hand.

11 When thou with rebukes dost correct man for iniquity, thou makest his beauty to consume away like a moth: surely every man is vanity. Selah.

12 Hear my prayer, O Lord, and give ear unto my cry; hold not thy peace at my tears: for I am a stranger with thee, and a sojourner, as all my fathers were.

13 O spare me, that I may recover strength, before I go hence, and be no more.

For Your Information

"Keep my mouth with a bridle": control his tongue.

"An handbreadth": the width of a hand. A poetic way of saying life is very short.

"Sojourner": alien.

Psalm 39

In an effort to refrain from sin, David decided to exercise restraint over his words. He chose to hold his tongue when troubles assailed him. But like most of us, he discovered that even stern discipline could not solve his spiritual woes. Though he did not speak, not even uttering good words, it did not end the spiritual dilemma. Inside, he burned with anger. Apart from the Holy Spirit's work in our lives, even our best efforts at obeying God are sure to fall short, as the psalmist learned.

Aware of the fragility of his own life, David asked God to make the best of the time he had in life. He recognized that his only hope lay in God and humbly asked for deliverance. Being corrected by God is a painful experience, but as the author to the Hebrews comments, God chastens those whom He loves (Hebrews 12:6).

Though he felt distant from God, David ended with hope that as his Lord's chastening ends, hope will revive.

- Have you shared David's struggle with words? Did you also begin to feel bitter about the situation? What would have been a better solution?

- Have you experienced God's chastening? Why did it hurt so much? What benefits did it bring to your life?

Psalm 40

1 I waited patiently for the Lord; and he inclined unto me, and heard my cry.

2 He brought me up also out of an horrible pit, out of the miry clay, and set my feet upon a rock, and established my goings.

3 And he hath put a new song in my mouth, even praise unto our God: many shall see it, and fear, and shall trust in the Lord.

4 Blessed is that man that maketh the Lord his trust, and respecteth not the proud, nor such as turn aside to lies.

5 Many, O Lord my God, are thy wonderful works which thou hast done, and thy thoughts which are to us-ward: they cannot be reckoned up in order unto thee: if I would declare and speak of them, they are more than can be numbered.

6 Sacrifice and offering thou didst not desire; mine ears hast thou opened: burnt offering and sin offering hast thou not required.

7 Then said I, Lo, I come: in the volume of the book it is written of me,

8 I delight to do thy will, O my God: yea, thy law is within my heart.

9 I have preached righteousness in the great congregation: lo, I have not refrained my lips, O Lord, thou knowest.

10 I have not hid thy righteousness within my heart; I have declared thy faithfulness and thy salvation: I have not concealed thy lovingkindness and thy truth from the great congregation.

11 Withhold not thou thy tender mercies from me, O Lord: let thy lovingkindness and thy truth continually preserve me.

12 For innumerable evils have compassed me about: mine iniquities have taken hold upon me, so that I am not able to look up; they are more than the hairs of mine head: therefore my heart faileth me.

13 Be pleased, O Lord, to deliver me: O Lord, make haste to help me.

14 Let them be ashamed and confounded together that seek after my soul to destroy it; let them be driven backward and put to shame that wish me evil.

15 Let them be desolate for a reward of their shame that say unto me, Aha, aha.

16 Let all those that seek thee rejoice and be glad in thee: let such as love thy salvation say continually, The Lord be magnified.

17 But I am poor and needy; yet the Lord thinketh upon me: thou art my help and my deliverer; make no tarrying, O my God.

For Your Information

"To us-ward": towards us.

"Reckoned up in order": God's blessings are too many to count.

"Offering thou didst not desire": The offering God really wants is a heart that is wholly His.

"Mine ears thou hast opened": Either his ears are opened to listen to God's truths, or his ear is pierced with an awl, which indicated he was a lifelong slave.

"Burnt offering and sin offering": two types of offerings made in the Old Testament period for forgiveness of sin. The offerings of that era prefigure the sacrifice of Christ, which they symbolize.

"In the volume of the book it is written of me": Bible commentators think this is a reference to scripture.

"Thy law is within my heart": He has internalized God's law, and it is a part of him.

"Aha, aha": the mocking sounds of his enemies.

Psalm 40

Because God heard David in his troubles and rescued him, the psalmist sings forth His praises and recommends that others trust Him too. Unlimited adulation and thanks are due to the Lord who saved him.

On the basis of his faith and his witness to God's faithfulness, the psalmist asks his Lord to continue to preserve him. David admits his own sin has, at least in part, caused this need for God's protection; now the evil he faces overwhelms his spirit and casts down hope. As his enemies attack, once again the king turns to God for aid and prays that those who stand against him will not receive the reward of seeing him fail.

Humbly, the psalmist admits his own spiritual emptiness, but his hope lies in the God who has not forgotten him. He asks God to rescue him yet again.

- Name some spiritual and physical ways in which God has rescued you. Have you praised Him for them? You may want to spend time doing that now.

- Has God rescued you from your own mistakes? How did your life change because of that? Did your attitude towards God alter too?

Psalm 41

1 Blessed is he that considereth the poor: the Lord will deliver him in time of trouble.

2 The Lord will preserve him, and keep him alive; and he shall be blessed upon the earth: and thou wilt not deliver him unto the will of his enemies.

3 The Lord will strengthen him upon the bed of languishing: thou wilt make all his bed in his sickness.

4 I said, Lord, be merciful unto me: heal my soul; for I have sinned against thee.

5 Mine enemies speak evil of me, When shall he die, and his name perish?

6 And if he come to see me, he speaketh vanity: his heart gathereth iniquity to itself; when he goeth abroad, he telleth it.

7 All that hate me whisper together against me: against me do they devise my hurt.

8 An evil disease, say they, cleaveth fast unto him: and now that he lieth he shall rise up no more.

9 Yea, mine own familiar friend, in whom I trusted, which did eat of my bread, hath lifted up his heel against me.

10 But thou, O Lord, be merciful unto me, and raise me up, that I may requite them.

11 By this I know that thou favourest me, because mine enemy doth not triumph over me.

12 And as for me, thou upholdest me in mine integrity, and settest me before thy face for ever.

13 Blessed be the Lord God of Israel from everlasting, and to everlasting. Amen, and Amen.

For Your Information

"Poor": This may refer to David, who is poor in spirit, or to those who have few physical resources.

"Shall be blessed upon the earth": shall receive temporal blessings.

"Bed of languishing": sickbed.

"His name perish": his name (and thus he) will not be remembered.

Ironically, David's critics' names are largely not remembered, while he is known as Israel's greatest king.

"An evil disease": Literally translated, it is "a thing of Belial [Satan]." His enemies slander him, saying sin and his unrepentant heart have caused his illness.

"My own familiar friend": This may be a reference to Ahitophel, David's prime minister, who betrayed him when David's son Absalom tried to take the throne. Jesus also identifies this as a prophecy of Judas' betrayal (John 13:18).

"Lifted up his heel": scornfully kicked.

"Requite": repay.

Psalm 41

In his illness, David cries out to God, declaring God's faithfulness and his own need for divine protection and healing. Confessing his sin, he pleads that his enemies might not be able to gloat over his death. In verses 4–9, he continues the complaint begun in former psalms against his slanderous enemies, one of whom is a former friend, for even as David is ill, they spread gossip, blaming him for imagined wrongs.

But David's hope lies not in his enemies or friends. He trusts in God, and asks that He will raise him up to fight again. Previously God has not allowed the king's enemies to triumph over him, and he trusts divine intervention will again uphold him.

This psalm, which closes the first of five books in the Psalms, fittingly ends with a glorious praise to the eternal Lord.

• In the midst of great suffering, David praised God. What did he focus on in this series of psalms? Can that help you praise Him, when you suffer?

• When someone wrongs you, do you want to extract vengeance? Does God want you to react in vengeance? (Read Romans 12:19.)

WEEK FIVE

Introduction

This week, the psalms we'll cover go from sheer, exuberant praise to human doubt at God's seeming lack of response. They vary from believers' deep trust and confidence to God's painful confrontation of His unfaithful people over their sins.

Spiritual life differs from day to day. Some days, we feel confident; other days, we wonder if God hears our prayers at all, and we question why He feels so distant. The psalmists encountered these feelings, too, and their writings reflect those emotions.

But none of those reactions mean that God changed. Over and over the psalms speak of God's covenant with His people. Historically, Middle Eastern nations formed agreements between each other. God used these written promises stating what each party would do as a picture of the relationship He had with His people. In Genesis 15, God also made a covenant of blood. In the Old Testament era, after a covenant promise between two countries was created, it was ratified by an animal sacrifice. After the sacrifice, the parties to the covenant passed between the halves of the animals. But there was one great difference in God's covenant. In Genesis 15, God alone passed through the sacrifice, symbolizing His unconditional promise: Even when they are unfaithful, He will never leave or forsake His people.

But God's covenant required the people to obey Him. When their sin temporarily broke the relationship, He became distanced from His people. When they continued in disobedience, He did not force Himself on them. Yet God never altered in His love for Israel. Always He called them back from sin, into love and submission to His will.

Over time, God expanded His promises. He began the promise to Abraham, who obeyed Him and moved to a new land (Genesis 12). God promised to make of the descendants of Abraham and his wife, Sarah, a new, blessed nation. Later, He renewed the promise with Moses and the people of the Exodus (Exodus 19). In the final Old Testament covenant, He created a kingly line with David, establishing the line of the Messiah (2 Samuel 7:16).

The new covenant, predicted by Jeremiah (Jeremiah 31:33), is fulfilled in the New Testament. With Jesus' sacrifice, all the Old Testament Messianic promises are accomplished. Jesus' death and resurrection replace animal sacrifices and give believers new hearts. The Holy Spirit came to indwell them, permanently changing hearts and minds (Acts 2:4; Ephesians 1:13; 1 Thessalonians 4:8).

But Christians still experience all the feelings David and the other psalmists wrote about in Psalms. Spiritual life has its ups and downs. We too have days when we intimately relate to God, and others when sin darkens our spiritual lives. But no matter how we feel, like the psalmists, we trust that God will never change.

Psalm 42

1 As the hart panteth after the water brooks, so panteth my soul after thee, O God.

2 My soul thirsteth for God, for the living God: when shall I come and appear before God?

3 My tears have been my meat day and night; while they continually say unto me, Where is thy God?

4 When I remember these things, I pour out my soul in me: for I had gone with the multitude, I went with them to the house of God, with the voice of joy and praise, with a multitude that kept holyday.

5 Why art thou cast down, O my soul? and why art thou disquieted in me? hope thou in God: for I shall yet praise him for the help of his countenance.

6 O my God, my soul is cast down within me: therefore will I remember thee from the land of Jordan, and of the Hermonites, from the hill Mizar.

7 Deep calleth unto deep at the noise of thy waterspouts: all thy waves and thy billows are gone over me.

8 Yet the Lord will command his lovingkindness in the daytime, and in the night his song shall be with me, and my prayer unto the God of my life.

9 I will say unto God my rock, Why hast thou forgotten me? why go I mourning because of the oppression of the enemy?

10 As with a sword in my bones, mine enemies reproach me; while they say daily unto me, Where is thy God?

11 Why art thou cast down, O my soul? and why art thou disquieted within me? hope thou in God: for I shall yet praise him, who is the health of my countenance, and my God.

Psalm 43

1 Judge me, O God, and plead my cause against an ungodly nation: O deliver me from the deceitful and unjust man.

2 For thou art the God of my strength: why dost thou cast me off? why go I mourning because of the oppression of the enemy?

3 O send out thy light and thy truth: let them lead me; let them bring me unto thy holy hill, and to thy tabernacles.

4 Then will I go unto the altar of God, unto God my exceeding joy: yea, upon the harp will I praise thee, O God my God.

5 Why art thou cast down, O my soul? and why art thou disquieted within me? hope in God: for I shall yet praise him, who is the health of my countenance, and my God.

For Your Information

"Panteth": desires desperately.

"Appear before God": in the temple.

"My tears have been my meat": I have fed on tears.

"Holyday": festival.

"His countenance": His presence.

"Waterspouts": waterfalls.

"Cast down": saddened.

"Health of my countenance": As a happy face appears cheerful, hope in God makes the psalmist joyful.

"Judge me": prove me innocent. The psalmist knows he is not guilty and asks God to prove it.

Psalm 42

Some scholars think this was a psalm of David, though the superscription does not specify it. Written for the temple singers, the psalm expresses the writer's desire to worship in Jerusalem's temple. Separated from his homeland and its holy festivals, the psalmist fondly remembers them.

But he need not be despondent, for even if temple worship is not possible, God remains with the psalmist. Despite his current sorrow, he will yet praise God, who will bring him joy again.

• Have you felt this kind of passionate desire to be close to God? Did it relate to where you worshiped? Does God have to be worshiped in a special place? What is required for real worship?

Psalm 43

Scholars consider this orphan psalm a continuation of the previous one. Certainly the same ideas appear here. In some cases words from the previous psalm are even repeated.

The psalmist calls upon God for His judgment in the case between him and his enemies of an ungodly nation. Trusting in God, he recognizes he need not feel downcast, for who is greater than God? So the psalmist seeks his Lord's guidance. He wants to go to Jerusalem and praise his Lord at the altar.

Finally the writer speaks to his soul, reminding himself that God will yet be praised and will lift him up.

• Have situations made you feel downcast? Were they greater than God? Did you really have to be discouraged by them? How would David recommend that you respond when you feel down?

Psalm 44

1 We have heard with our ears, O God, our fathers have told us, what work thou didst in their days, in the times of old.

2 How thou didst drive out the heathen with thy hand, and plantedst them; how thou didst afflict the people, and cast them out.

3 For they got not the land in possession by their own sword, neither did their own arm save them: but thy right hand, and thine arm, and the light of thy countenance, because thou hadst a favour unto them.

4 Thou art my King, O God: command deliverances for Jacob.

5 Through thee will we push down our enemies: through thy name will we tread them under that rise up against us.

6 For I will not trust in my bow, neither shall my sword save me.

7 But thou hast saved us from our enemies, and hast put them to shame that hated us.

8 In God we boast all the day long, and praise thy name for ever. Selah.

9 But thou hast cast off, and put us to shame; and goest not forth with our armies.

10 Thou makest us to turn back from the enemy: and they which hate us spoil for themselves.

11 Thou hast given us like sheep appointed for meat; and hast scattered us among the heathen.

12 Thou sellest thy people for nought, and dost not increase thy wealth by their price.

13 Thou makest us a reproach to our neighbours, a scorn and a derision to them that are round about us.

14 Thou makest us a byword among the heathen, a shaking of the head among the people.

15 My confusion is continually before me, and the shame of my face hath covered me,

16 For the voice of him that reproacheth and blasphemeth; by reason of the enemy and avenger.

17 All this is come upon us; yet have we not forgotten thee, neither have we dealt falsely in thy covenant.

18 Our heart is not turned back, neither have our steps declined from thy way;

19 Though thou hast sore broken us in the place of dragons, and covered us with the shadow of death.

20 If we have forgotten the name of our God, or stretched out our hands to a strange God;

21 Shall not God search this out? for he knoweth the secrets of the heart.

22 Yea, for thy sake are we killed all the day long; we are counted as sheep for the slaughter.

23 Awake, why sleepest thou, O Lord? arise, cast us not off for ever.

24 Wherefore hidest thou thy face, and forgettest our affliction and our oppression?

25 For our soul is bowed down to the dust: our belly cleaveth unto the earth.

26 Arise for our help, and redeem us for thy mercies' sake.

For Your Information
"Jacob": Israel.

"Through thy name": by Your power (A name has authority, when it's of an important one).

"Goest not forth with our armies": When God went out with Israel's army, they won. When He did not join them, they lost.

"Spoil for themselves": take plunder from us.

"For the voice of him that reproacheth and blasphemeth": the psalmist's enemy heaps reproaches on him and blasphemes God.

"Stretched out our hands": worshiped.

"Sheep": a picture of helplessness.

Psalm 44
The writer and situation of this psalm are unknown, but it speaks to a time when the nation faced loss of stature and power. In the past, God had brought victory—the psalmist is well aware of that history and the

need to trust in God, instead of a sword. But though he and his nation praise God, the victories do not come. They army retreats and sees the land plundered.

The psalmist wonders why this happened, though the people did not lose faith. He would understand, if they had been faithless, but they stood firm. So he calls on God for his nation, asking him to remember and rescue them, out of His love.

• Have you faced situations in which God did not seem to rescue you? How did you respond to such tests of faith? Was God faithful to you, even in this?

• Does a lack of response mean that God no longer cares? That He will not rescue us? How can we know this?

Psalm 45

1 My heart is inditing a good matter: I speak of the things which I have made touching the king: my tongue is the pen of a ready writer.

2 Thou art fairer than the children of men: grace is poured into thy lips: therefore God hath blessed thee for ever.

3 Gird thy sword upon thy thigh, O most mighty, with thy glory and thy majesty.

4 And in thy majesty ride prosperously because of truth and meekness and righteousness; and thy right hand shall teach thee terrible things.

5 Thine arrows are sharp in the heart of the king's enemies; whereby the people fall under thee.

6 Thy throne, O God, is for ever and ever: the sceptre of thy kingdom is a right sceptre.

7 Thou lovest righteousness, and hatest wickedness: therefore God, thy God, hath anointed thee with the oil of gladness above thy fellows.

8 All thy garments smell of myrrh, and aloes, and cassia, out of the ivory palaces, whereby they have made thee glad.

9 Kings' daughters were among thy honourable women: upon thy right hand did stand the queen in gold of Ophir.

10 Hearken, O daughter, and consider, and incline thine ear; forget also thine own people, and thy father's house;

11 So shall the king greatly desire thy beauty: for he is thy Lord; and worship thou him.

12 And the daughter of Tyre shall be there with a gift; even the rich among the people shall intreat thy favour.

13 The king's daughter is all glorious within: her clothing is of wrought gold.

14 She shall be brought unto the king in raiment of needlework: the virgins her companions that follow her shall be brought unto thee.

15 With gladness and rejoicing shall they be brought: they shall enter into the king's palace.

16 Instead of thy fathers shall be thy children, whom thou mayest make princes in all the earth.

17 I will make thy name to be remembered in all generations: therefore shall the people praise thee for ever and ever.

For Your Information
"Inditing": boiling up, as a fountain.

"Ride prosperously": conduct a victorious battle.

"Meekness and righteousness": The king will rule rightly, making a good government.

"Oil of gladness": a symbol of joy.

"Myrrh, and aloes, and cassia": rare, expensive, and fragrant spices.

"Gold of Ophir": Her robes are woven with gold thread or have ornaments of gold.

"Daughter of Tyre": a personification of the wealthy Phoenician city of Tyre, with which David's dynasty traded. This is also a picture of the Gentiles honoring Christ.

"Brought unto the king": She is brought to the king's home, as the marriage custom dictated.

Psalm 45

As a Messianic psalm, this is both a wedding song for a king of David's line and praise for the kingly Messiah, coming in power to claim His bride, the church.

The psalmist is stirred by his subject into skillful words and begins with praise for the king. He appears majestic on his wedding day, as befits an international figure who has conquered nations and rules justly.

Prophetically this also speaks of the Messiah, who is "fairer than the children of men," because he is beautiful to those who have accepted His sacrifice. No one has done more for them, and He deserves such praise. As a warrior, He will come to free His bride (Revelation 19:11).

Verses 9–13 focus on the richly dressed bride, who attracts the king with her beauty. She is a picture of the church, for whom Christ died. Sanctified, now she joins him, reflecting His glory. With rejoicing, they enter the heavenly places.

Finally, God promises Jesus' name shall be remembered throughout the generations, and He shall be eternally praised.

• Do you see Christ's glory in this way? What does it mean for you? How can it affect your life?

Psalm 46

1 God is our refuge and strength, a very present help in trouble.

2 Therefore will not we fear, though the earth be removed, and though the mountains be carried into the midst of the sea;

3 Though the waters thereof roar and be troubled, though the mountains shake with the swelling thereof. Selah.

4 There is a river, the streams whereof shall make glad the city of God, the holy place of the tabernacles of the most High.

5 God is in the midst of her; she shall not be moved: God shall help her, and that right early.

6 The heathen raged, the kingdoms were moved: he uttered his voice, the earth melted.

7 The Lord of hosts is with us; the God of Jacob is our refuge. Selah.

8 Come, behold the works of the Lord, what desolations he hath made in the earth.

9 He maketh wars to cease unto the end of the earth; he breaketh the bow, and cutteth the spear in sunder; he burneth the chariot in the fire.

10 Be still, and know that I am God: I will be exalted among the heathen, I will be exalted in the earth.

11 The Lord of hosts is with us; the God of Jacob is our refuge. Selah.

Psalm 47

1 O clap your hands, all ye people; shout unto God with the voice of triumph.

2 For the Lord most high is terrible; he is a great King over all the earth.

3 He shall subdue the people under us, and the nations under our feet.

4 He shall choose our inheritance for us, the excellency of Jacob whom he loved. Selah.

5 God is gone up with a shout, the Lord with the sound of a trumpet.

6 Sing praises to God, sing praises: sing praises unto our King, sing praises.

7 For God is the King of all the earth: sing ye praises with understanding.

8 God reigneth over the heathen: God sitteth upon the throne of his holiness.

9 The princes of the people are gathered together, even the people of the God of Abraham: for the shields of the earth belong unto God: he is greatly exalted.

For Your Information

"River": Often this is seen as being God Himself.

"Make glad the city of God": gladden the hearts of the people of His city because this peaceful river provides for them.

"Most High": Sovereign God.

"Right early": at daybreak.

"Lord of hosts": God as the Lord of creation, another way of referring to His sovereignty.

"In sunder": apart.

"Clap your hands": a sign of rejoicing.

"Throne of his holiness": the holy of holiness, the holiest part of the temple.

"Shields": the princes, who shielded their lands from harm.

Psalm 46

No matter what Israel faces, this unnamed psalmist encourages the nation to seek God's help. Though the very earth be destroyed, He is still their only refuge, the sole strength of His people.

God will provide for His people, who are pictured by the city of God. His holy tabernacle, symbolic of His own presence, is in the midst of them. The destruction of unbelievers by God's power is promised. Then all wars will end, and He will be glorified as Lord.

- Is God your refuge? What does that mean to you? What has He protected you from?

Psalm 47

God as King is the subject of this psalm that calls on people of all nations to rejoice in His sovereignty. He is pictured as a powerful potentate. Ultimately those who believe in him prove victorious over the unbelievers.

Verse 5 has a Messianic meaning, referring to Christ's ascension to heaven. In the Old Testament era, it might also have referred to David's celebration as the Ark of the Covenant was carried to Jerusalem (2 Samuel 6).

The psalmist renews his call for worship of the King, who in His holiness reigns over all, both faithful and unbelieving. Isaiah 45:23 speaks of this more directly when God promises that before Him every knee will bow and every tongue swear. Paul ascribes these verses to Jesus in Philippians 2:10–11.

- Do you look forward to a day when God will rule all? How can you know He will fulfill this promise?

Psalm 48

1 Great is the Lord, and greatly to be praised in the city of our God, in the mountain of his holiness.

2 Beautiful for situation, the joy of the whole earth, is mount Zion, on the sides of the north, the city of the great King.

3 God is known in her palaces for a refuge.

4 For, lo, the kings were assembled, they passed by together.

5 They saw it, and so they marvelled; they were troubled, and hasted away.

6 Fear took hold upon them there, and pain, as of a woman in travail.

7 Thou breakest the ships of Tarshish with an east wind.

8 As we have heard, so have we seen in the city of the Lord of hosts, in the city of our God: God will establish it for ever. Selah.

9 We have thought of thy lovingkindness, O God, in the midst of thy temple.

10 According to thy name, O God, so is thy praise unto the ends of the earth: thy right hand is full of righteousness.

11 Let mount Zion rejoice, let the daughters of Judah be glad, because of thy judgments.

12 Walk about Zion, and go round about her: tell the towers thereof.

13 Mark ye well her bulwarks, consider her palaces; that ye may tell it to the generation following.

14 For this God is our God for ever and ever: he will be our guide even unto death.

Psalm 52

1 Why boastest thou thyself in mischief, O mighty man? the goodness of God endureth continually.

2 Thy tongue deviseth mischiefs; like a sharp razor, working deceitfully.

3 Thou lovest evil more than good; and lying rather than to speak righteousness. Selah.

4 Thou lovest all devouring words, O thou deceitful tongue.

5 God shall likewise destroy thee for ever, he shall take thee away, and pluck thee out of thy dwelling place, and root thee out of the

land of the living. Selah.

6 The righteous also shall see, and fear, and shall laugh at him:

7 Lo, this is the man that made not God his strength; but trusted in the abundance of his riches, and strengthened himself in his wickedness.

8 But I am like a green olive tree in the house of God: I trust in the mercy of God for ever and ever.

9 I will praise thee for ever, because thou hast done it: and I will wait on thy name; for it is good before thy saints.

For Your Information

"Situation": elevation.

"Travail": childbirth.

"Ships of Tarshish": trading vessels from a distant land, carrying valuable refined metals.

"The daughters of Judah": the people.

"Green olive tree": a strong, young tree that will live for hundreds or years.

Psalm 48

The impregnable city of Jerusalem, site of the worship of God, is the focus for this psalm glorifying the power of God. Through describing the holy city, the psalmist simultaneously shows the power of its deity.

Awed, the armies that march against Jerusalem turn and run away in fear. The psalmist praises God for His eternal protection of His city, and thus His people. He calls on the people to spread the news of God's faithfulness as a protector and declares that He will guide them forever.

• How have you seen God's power of protection over you? Has it awed you? Could anything remove His protection from you?

Psalm 52

This psalm was written after the incidents described in 1 Samuel 21–22 occurred. David ran from King Saul, in fear of his life, and sought the aide of the priests of Nob. Doeg the Edomite told Saul about it, and Saul had him kill the priests. In response, David penned this psalm about the wicked betrayer.

Verses 1–4 describe Doeg and the evil attitudes that clearly show his sin. But David is certain God will bring about justice and destroy him. Finally, the psalmist describes his own trust in God. While Doeg will die, David will flourish with God for eternity.

• When someone does evil to you, are you quick to seek retribution, or do you follow David's example and ask God to make things right? Could you improve on God's ability to bring about justice?

Psalm 49

1 Hear this, all ye people; give ear, all ye inhabitants of the world:

2 Both low and high, rich and poor, together.

3 My mouth shall speak of wisdom; and the meditation of my heart shall be of understanding.

4 I will incline mine ear to a parable: I will open my dark saying upon the harp.

5 Wherefore should I fear in the days of evil, when the iniquity of my heels shall compass me about?

6 They that trust in their wealth, and boast themselves in the multitude of their riches;

7 None of them can by any means redeem his brother, nor give to God a ransom for him:

8 (For the redemption of their soul is precious, and it ceaseth for ever:)

9 That he should still live for ever, and not see corruption.

10 For he seeth that wise men die, likewise the fool and the brutish person perish, and leave their wealth to others.

11 Their inward thought is, that their houses shall continue for ever, and their dwelling places to all generations; they call their lands after their own names.

12 Nevertheless man being in honour abideth not: he is like the beasts that perish.

13 This their way is their folly: yet their posterity approve their sayings. Selah.

14 Like sheep they are laid in the grave; death shall feed on them; and the upright shall have dominion over them in the morning; and their beauty shall consume in the grave from their dwelling.

15 But God will redeem my soul from the power of the grave: for he shall receive me. Selah.

16 Be not thou afraid when one is made rich, when the glory of his house is increased;

17 For when he dieth he shall carry nothing away: his glory shall not descend after him.

18 Though while he lived he blessed his soul: and men will praise thee, when thou doest well to thyself.

19 He shall go to the generation of his fathers; they shall never see light.

20 Man that is in honour, and understandeth not, is like the beasts that perish.

For Your Information
"Incline": listen attentively.

"Parable": a wise teaching.

"Open": disclose.

"Dark saying": riddle.

"Harp": the psalmist's accompaniment.

"The iniquity of my heels": something that trips up the psalmist.

"It ceaseth for ever": The price of salvation is too costly for a human to pay it.

"Like the beasts that perish": They leave nothing behind them. (See also the reference in verse 14 to sheep.)

"Corruption": death.

"Dominion": authority.

"Though while he lived he blessed his soul": During his lifetime, he thought himself happy.

"Light": God (compare to Psalms 27:1).

Psalm 49
This teaching psalm summons all people to trust in God. The first four verses, the introductory call, explain the psalmist's purpose. The next two compare the trusting psalmist, a picture of the faithful person, to those who put their confidence in wealth.

No human has power to redeem a soul, which is precious beyond earthly price; nor can a person make it live for eternity. All people die and leave their earthly goods to others. Expecting to "take it with you" is foolish, yet many fall for that trap. Even facing the reality of death often does not stop such weak thinking.

But God has the power to redeem. So when a believer sees the sinful person becoming rich in the goods of this world, it is not time to despair. The faithful miss out on nothing, since physical blessings cannot follow the soul into eternity. In the end, the unbelieving soul that had many possessions will not own Christ. Without spiritual understanding, the soul is lost.

- Has it upset you that some people who live immorally own so many possessions? What role do physical things play in God's blessings? Are they His greatest blessing?

- Why could only Jesus pay the price for a soul?

Psalm 50

1 The mighty God, even the Lord, hath spoken, and called the earth from the rising of the sun unto the going down thereof.

2 Out of Zion, the perfection of beauty, God hath shined.

3 Our God shall come, and shall not keep silence: a fire shall devour before him, and it shall be very tempestuous round about him.

4 He shall call to the heavens from above, and to the earth, that he may judge his people.

5 Gather my saints together unto me; those that have made a covenant with me by sacrifice.

6 And the heavens shall declare his righteousness: for God is judge himself. Selah.

7 Hear, O my people, and I will speak; O Israel, and I will testify against thee: I am God, even thy God.

8 I will not reprove thee for thy sacrifices or thy burnt offerings to have been continually before me.

9 I will take no bullock out of thy house, nor he goats out of thy folds.

10 For every beast of the forest is mine, and the cattle upon a thousand hills.

11 I know all the fowls of the mountains: and the wild beasts of the field are mine.

12 If I were hungry, I would not tell thee: for the world is mine, and the fulness thereof.

13 Will I eat the flesh of bulls, or drink the blood of goats?

14 Offer unto God thanksgiving; and pay thy vows unto the most High:

15 And call upon me in the day of trouble: I will deliver thee, and thou shalt glorify me.

16 But unto the wicked God saith, What hast thou to do to declare my statutes, or that thou shouldest take my covenant in thy mouth?

17 Seeing thou hatest instruction, and castest my words behind thee.

18 When thou sawest a thief, then thou consentedst with him, and hast been partaker with adulterers.

19 Thou givest thy mouth to evil, and thy tongue frameth deceit.

20 Thou sittest and speakest against thy brother; thou slanderest thine own mother's son.

21 These things hast thou done, and I kept silence; thou thought-est that I was altogether such an one as thyself: but I will reprove thee, and set them in order before thine eyes.

22 Now consider this, ye that forget God, lest I tear you in pieces, and there be none to deliver.

23 Whoso offereth praise glorifieth me: and to him that ordereth his conversation aright will I shew the salvation of God.

For Your Information

"Perfection of beauty": The city is beautiful because it is holy.

"Saints": holy ones, those with faith in God.

"Bullock": young bull.

Psalm 50

God comes to confront His people in judgment. The first six verses of the psalm show Him in all His glory, holding His people to account and correcting their actions, which have fallen far short of their covenant.

Verses 7–15 describe the error of the Israelites, who have failed to understand what God requires. They have not adequately burned sac-rifices to Him, but even more, they have not understood the meaning of the offerings. It is not sacrifice of the beasts that is important to God, but the dedication of the heart that they symbolize. God wants people to turn to Him, to seek deliverance, and praise His glory.

Finally, God speaks to those with no faith. They have pretended to be part of His covenant people, but have hated all God commanded of them. Instead of following His laws, they have willingly fallen in with sinners and taken part in sin themselves. God did not correct them, so they decided they had His approval. But now He's offering that cor-rection. He calls on the wicked to turn, before they are destroyed, and promises that only those who glorify Him will be saved.

• Which is more important to God—a burnt offering or a heart offering? Why? Since there are no burnt offerings today, what would compare with that? What would show a heart offering?

- Why do unbelievers believe God approves of them? Does He? What keeps them from knowing the truth?

- What kinds of sacrifice are you offering to God? Are there any you need to offer?

WEEK SIX

Introduction

All the psalms for this week are attributed to David.

In Psalm 51, we see David's repentance following his sin with Bathsheba (2 Samuel 11). Aware of God's faithfulness and his own lack of it, he painfully casts himself on the Redeemer. In these verses we get an honest look at the results of sin in his life. Perhaps the psalmist kept in mind the fate of King Saul, whom God denied forgiveness because he was not truly sorry for his wrongdoing (1 Samuel 15). That this king's repentance was sincere we know both by his words here and by his later life: He does not repeat these errors.

Obviously certain spiritual truths were hallmarks for David. Like all of us, some experiences and needs occurred more than once in his life, and he repeatedly brought them before God. It is not that God did not know or care about these situations, but He was working out a plan that included David's continued faithfulness. The psalms David wrote reflected what God was doing in his life.

Psalm 53 is actually largely repetitive of an earlier psalm. God does repeat His truths in scripture, not because He has forgotten what was already committed to its pages, but because we often need to revisit these realities. Even those who are faithful sometimes need to return to a familiar truth. So when we see a repetition in God's Word, we should not ignore it, but be especially attentive.

Repeatedly we see David return to the theme of God's ability to save the believer from enemies. After Saul's fall from God's grace, the prophet Samuel anointed David king, on God's command. But the change in authority was not immediate. Saul stayed in power for a time and tried to rid himself of the newly anointed contender for the throne. Yet David never fought Saul—he only fled from his soldiers repeatedly and continually asked God to protect him. David trusted God to deal with Saul and his men, because he wanted to remain godly. Though anointed in Saul's place, David did not feel free to attack him and repeatedly reminded others that Saul was God's anointed. Not until Saul committed suicide, following a battle with the Philistines (1 Samuel 31), was David crowned king.

Through all his trials, God never let David down; the newly anointed king was never captured or killed by his enemies. David's repeated self-assurances that God will protect him are prophetic, as well as a sign of his own beliefs.

The truths David experienced have not changed in the thousands of years since he penned them. God still protects those who stubbornly trust in Him for deliverance. We may not be seeking a throne, but as we attempt to remain faithful, God will see us through our trials and troubles. The One who was faithful for David has not changed His nature. We can rely on Him in all we do.

Psalm 51

1 Have mercy upon me, O God, according to thy lovingkindness: according unto the multitude of thy tender mercies blot out my transgressions.

2 Wash me throughly from mine iniquity, and cleanse me from my sin.

3 For I acknowledge my transgressions: and my sin is ever before me.

4 Against thee, thee only, have I sinned, and done this evil in thy sight: that thou mightest be justified when thou speakest, and be clear when thou Judgest.

5 Behold, I was shapen in iniquity; and in sin did my mother conceive me.

6 Behold, thou desirest truth in the inward parts: and in the hidden part thou shalt make me to know wisdom.

7 Purge me with hyssop, and I shall be clean: wash me, and I shall be whiter than snow.

8 Make me to hear joy and gladness; that the bones which thou hast broken may rejoice.

9 Hide thy face from my sins, and blot out all mine iniquities.

10 Create in me a clean heart, O God; and renew a right spirit within me.

11 Cast me not away from thy presence; and take not thy holy spirit from me.

12 Restore unto me the joy of thy salvation; and uphold me with thy free spirit.

13 Then will I teach transgressors thy ways; and sinners shall be converted unto thee.

14 Deliver me from bloodguiltiness, O God, thou God of my salvation: and my tongue shall sing aloud of thy righteousness.

15 O Lord, open thou my lips; and my mouth shall shew forth thy praise.

16 For thou desirest not sacrifice; else would I give it: thou delightest not in burnt offering.

17 The sacrifices of God are a broken spirit: a broken and a contrite heart, O God, thou wilt not despise.

18 Do good in thy good pleasure unto Zion: build thou the walls of Jerusalem.

19 Then shalt thou be pleased with the sacrifices of righteousness, with burnt offering and whole burnt offering: then shall they offer bullocks upon thine altar.

For Your Information

"Lovingkindness": God's unfailing love for His people, despite their failures. He bases His love on His covenant promise, not their ability to obey.

"Shapen": shaped.

"Inward parts": his deepest being.

"Hyssop": a small plant symbolizing humility, used to sprinkle sacrificial blood. It symbolizes David's desire to be cleansed from sin.

"Bones which thou hast broken": the damage of sin hurts like a bodily pain.

"Bloodguiltiness": guilt for murder (see 2 Samuel 11:14–17).

"The sacrifices of righteousness": More important than a burnt offering is the sacrifice a person makes by giving up sin and doing God's will.

Psalm 51

Second Samuel 11 describes the incidents David atoned for in these verses. He became sexually involved with a married woman, Bathsheba, and plotted to kill her husband when she became pregnant. Then the prophet Nathan confronted the king with his sin (2 Samuel 12), and David repented.

David clearly acknowledges his own sin and asks God's mercy (verses 1–6), accepting the truth that he transgressed God's laws. He requests that He cleanse him, because he knows only God can provide atonement. As God makes the sin right, through His forgiveness, David rejoices. His heart and spirit are broken, open to correction, and God does not despise him. David's heart and soul sacrifice is acceptable, and he can again offer a bull as an offering, to signify his spiritual change.

- Why is a heart change better than a burnt offering? What does that offering symbolize?

- Does a believer have to sin in the ways David did to feel such spiritual sorrow? Must another human confront the sinner to make the sin obvious?

Psalm 53

1 The fool hath said in his heart, There is no God. Corrupt are they, and have done abominable iniquity: there is none that doeth good.

2 God looked down from heaven upon the children of men, to see if there were any that did understand, that did seek God.

3 Every one of them is gone back: they are altogether become filthy; there is none that doeth good, no, not one.

4 Have the workers of iniquity no knowledge? who eat up my people as they eat bread: they have not called upon God.

5 There were they in great fear, where no fear was: for God hath scattered the bones of him that encampeth against thee: thou hast put them to shame, because God hath despised them.

6 Oh that the salvation of Israel were come out of Zion! When God bringeth back the captivity of his people, Jacob shall rejoice, and Israel shall be glad.

Psalm 56

1 Be merciful unto me, O God: for man would swallow me up; he fighting daily oppresseth me.

2 Mine enemies would daily swallow me up: for they be many that fight against me, O thou most High.

3 What time I am afraid, I will trust in thee.

4 In God I will praise his word, in God I have put my trust; I will not fear what flesh can do unto me.

5 Every day they wrest my words: all their thoughts are against me for evil.

6 They gather themselves together, they hide themselves, they mark my steps, when they wait for my soul.

7 Shall they escape by iniquity? in thine anger cast down the people, O God.

8 Thou tellest my wanderings: put thou my tears into thy bottle: are they not in thy book?

9 When I cry unto thee, then shall mine enemies turn back: this I know; for God is for me.

10 In God will I praise his word: in the Lord will I praise his word.

11 In God have I put my trust: I will not be afraid what man can do unto me.

12 Thy vows are upon me, O God: I will render praises unto thee.

13 For thou hast delivered my soul from death: wilt not thou deliver my feet from falling, that I may walk before God in the light of the living?

For Your Information

"Wrest": twist.

"Mark my steps": watch what I do.

"Scattered the bones": as an enemy whose fallen are not buried. They lie on the field and decay.

"Flesh": men.

Psalm 53

If this psalm seems rather familiar, don't be surprised. It is almost identical to Psalm 14. Perhaps the repetition of these truths is necessary because humanity is so prone to discounting and denying God.

There are minor differences with Psalm 14, up to and after verse 5 In that verse, the psalmist draws a picture of the destruction God brings upon His enemies. Because He despises the enemy, God brings them to such an awful destruction.

• Why do you think God chose this psalm to be essentially repeated in the psalms? Remember that He has a purpose for everything in His Word. Compare the differences you find between this psalm and Psalm 14.

Psalm 56

David, running from King Saul in fear of his life, left the priests at Nob (see Psalm 52) and fled to Gath, home of his enemies the Philistines. First Samuel 21:10–15 describes the events that took place there. Still in fear, David pretended to be insane, so the Philistines would not kill him. Their king could not wait to see David gone, and he left unharmed.

In these verses, the psalmist cries out for mercy, as he fears those who constantly attack him both verbally and physically. He promises his Lord trust and praise, then numbers his complaints against his enemies. *Should the wicked escape punishment?* he asks. Yet God has not forgotten, he is aware of all David's sorrow and has recorded it.

Finally, he confesses that his own cries to God will bring God's response. As David trusts, God will surely save him. What man is greater than God?

- Why would God wait until David cried out to come to his rescue? Have you ever felt God waited to rescue you? Did His response come at the right time?

Psalm 54

1 Save me, O God, by thy name, and judge me by thy strength.

2 Hear my prayer, O God; give ear to the words of my mouth.

3 For strangers are risen up against me, and oppressors seek after my soul: they have not set God before them. Selah.

4 Behold, God is mine helper: the Lord is with them that uphold my soul.

5 He shall reward evil unto mine enemies: cut them off in thy truth.

6 I will freely sacrifice unto thee: I will praise thy name, O Lord; for it is good.

7 For he hath delivered me out of all trouble: and mine eye hath seen his desire upon mine enemies.

Psalm 57

1 Be merciful unto me, O God, be merciful unto me: for my soul trusteth in thee: yea, in the shadow of thy wings will I make my refuge, until these calamities be overpast.

2 I will cry unto God most high; unto God that performeth all things for me.

3 He shall send from heaven, and save me from the reproach of him that would swallow me up. Selah. God shall send forth his mercy and his truth.

4 My soul is among lions: and I lie even among them that are set on fire, even the sons of men, whose teeth are spears and arrows, and their tongue a sharp sword.

5 Be thou exalted, O God, above the heavens; let thy glory be above all the earth.

6 They have prepared a net for my steps; my soul is bowed down: they have digged a pit before me, into the midst whereof they are fallen themselves. Selah.

7 My heart is fixed, O God, my heart is fixed: I will sing and give praise.

8 Awake up, my glory; awake, psaltery and harp: I myself will awake early.

9 I will praise thee, O Lord, among the people: I will sing unto thee among the nations.

10 For thy mercy is great unto the heavens, and thy truth unto the clouds.

11 Be thou exalted, O God, above the heavens: let thy glory be above all the earth.

For Your Information

"Judge me by thy strength": David asks to be judged and vindicated by God's power.

"Strangers": the people of Ziph, who twice told Saul where David was hiding (1 Samuel 23:19–20; 26:1). Though Israelites, they were certainly estranged from God.

"Oppressors": a reference to Saul.

"Lions": David pictures the danger of his enemies.

"I lie": like a sheep among lions.

Psalm 54

Fleeing from Saul, this is the first of two times David will be betrayed by the people of Ziph (1 Samuel 23:19; 1 Samuel 26:1). Desperate, he continues running and praying for God's protection. Unable to trust anyone, David admitted he feared for his life at the hands of ruthless men. Obviously those who hounded him were spiritually far from God, or they would not have sought to kill His anointed. But David, trusting the Almighty, confidently expects help, not only for his soul, but in the salvation of his earthly life. God will continue to protect him from enemies, and for that David offers Him praise.

• God often provides extraordinary help in desperate situations. Have you experienced this? How did you respond?

Psalm 57

No matter where David goes, Saul follows. First Samuel 24 tells of a time when Saul came so near, though David was hiding in a cave, he was surreptitiously able to cut off a piece of his enemy's robe. Yet God protected His chosen one.

David praises God's mercy, that though helpless in his own power, he was protected from those who sought his death. Though his enemies hunted him like an animal, they have been caught in their own trap.

The psalmist closes by turning to joyous public praise, exalting the Lord who accomplishes such a feat.

• Is there any dire situation in which God would not help you? Does God help even when a Christian has fallen into sin? What does that person need to do?

Psalm 55

1 Give ear to my prayer, O God; and hide not thyself from my supplication.

2 Attend unto me, and hear me: I mourn in my complaint, and make a noise;

3 Because of the voice of the enemy, because of the oppression of the wicked: for they cast iniquity upon me, and in wrath they hate me.

4 My heart is sore pained within me: and the terrors of death are fallen upon me.

5 Fearfulness and trembling are come upon me, and horror hath overwhelmed me.

6 And I said, Oh that I had wings like a dove! for then would I fly away, and be at rest.

7 Lo, then would I wander far off, and remain in the wilderness. Selah.

8 I would hasten my escape from the windy storm and tempest.

9 Destroy, O Lord, and divide their tongues: for I have seen violence and strife in the city.

10 Day and night they go about it upon the walls thereof: mischief also and sorrow are in the midst of it.

11 Wickedness is in the midst thereof: deceit and guile depart not from her streets.

12 For it was not an enemy that reproached me; then I could have borne it: neither was it he that hated me that did magnify himself against me; then I would have hid myself from him:

13 But it was thou, a man mine equal, my guide, and mine acquaintance.

14 We took sweet counsel together, and walked unto the house of God in company.

15 Let death seize upon them, and let them go down quick into hell: for wickedness is in their dwellings, and among them.

16 As for me, I will call upon God; and the Lord shall save me.

17 Evening, and morning, and at noon, will I pray, and cry aloud: and he shall hear my voice.

18 He hath delivered my soul in peace from the battle that was against me: for there were many with me.

19 God shall hear, and afflict them, even he that abideth of old.

Selah. Because they have no changes, therefore they fear not God.

20 He hath put forth his hands against such as be at peace with him: he hath broken his covenant.

21 The words of his mouth were smoother than butter, but war was in his heart: his words were softer than oil, yet were they drawn swords.

22 Cast thy burden upon the Lord, and he shall sustain thee: he shall never suffer the righteous to be moved.

23 But thou, O God, shalt bring them down into the pit of destruction: bloody and deceitful men shall not live out half their days; but I will trust in thee.

For Your Information

"Terrors of death": fear of death.

"Wings like a dove": a picture of escape, not a literal desire.

"Day and night they go about it upon the walls thereof": They are like watchmen on the city walls, but according to the rest of the verse, they are treacherous.

"Acquaintance": In the original Hebrew, this indicated a closer relationship.

"No changes": Because they are prosperous, their spirits are hardened to God.

Psalm 55

Scholars think this psalm may have been written during Absalom's conspiracy to take David's throne. Though the superscription does not indicate it, the events would fit. Because it speaks of betrayal, this is also a Messianic psalm, predicting the betrayal of Christ by Judas.

David appeals to God to listen and outlines his case against the enemies (verses 1–3). Then he shares with God his fears and desires to escape them (verses 4–8) and provides details about the evil being done in his city and the betrayal taking place there.

Though David would like to see the betrayers dead, he leaves their punishment in God's hands, simply calling upon his Savior to deal with the situation. Bidding on all believers to cast their cares on God, the psalmist ends by expressing his own trust in the Lord's justice.

• No matter what David experiences, he is very honest with God. He tells him all he thinks and feels. Is that hard to do? Why?

• David is very certain God will bring about justice. How could he be so sure? Do you have equal reason to trust God?

Psalm 58

1 Do ye indeed speak righteousness, O congregation? do ye judge uprightly, O ye sons of men?

2 Yea, in heart ye work wickedness; ye weigh the violence of your hands in the earth.

3 The wicked are estranged from the womb: they go astray as soon as they be born, speaking lies.

4 Their poison is like the poison of a serpent: they are like the deaf adder that stoppeth her ear;

5 Which will not hearken to the voice of charmers, charming never so wisely.

6 Break their teeth, O God, in their mouth: break out the great teeth of the young lions, O Lord.

7 Let them melt away as waters which run continually: when he bendeth his bow to shoot his arrows, let them be as cut in pieces.

8 As a snail which melteth, let every one of them pass away: like the untimely birth of a woman, that they may not see the sun.

9 Before your pots can feel the thorns, he shall take them away as with a whirlwind, both living, and in his wrath.

10 The righteous shall rejoice when he seeth the vengeance: he shall wash his feet in the blood of the wicked.

11 So that a man shall say, Verily there is a reward for the righteous: verily he is a God that judgeth in the earth.

For Your Information

"Ye weigh the violence of your hands in the earth": You issue unjust decisions.

"Estranged from the womb": They are far from God their whole lives.

"Stoppeth her ear": cannot listen. They have sinned so long they can no longer hear God's truth.

"Charmers": snake charmers.

"As a snail which melteth": This speaks of the seeming melting movement of the snail.

"Thorns": Thornbush twigs were used for kindling.

"Wash his feet in the blood of the wicked": There shall be much
  bloodshed.

Psalm 58

Here David addresses himself to the wicked judges whose hearts and
hands pervert justice. From the moment they were born, they seem to
have put God at a distance: they lie, spread poison, and will not listen
to the Lord.

Calling out to God for justice, David asks him to defang these
lions and make them melt away as if they had never been. Those who
do not follow God do not last, and the psalmist trusts the Lord will use
the frailty of life against these enemies. Then the righteous will rejoice
in their destruction and in the Righteous Judge, their God.

• Why does God take justice so seriously? Is justice delayed necessarily
  a sign He will not provide it?

• As a king, why was it important for David to take justice seriously?
  How could he make his justice like God's?

• Why do the righteous rejoice in vengeance? Hint: Who provides the
  vengeance?

Psalm 59

1 Deliver me from mine enemies, O my God: defend me from them that rise up against me.

2 Deliver me from the workers of iniquity, and save me from bloody men.

3 For, lo, they lie in wait for my soul: the mighty are gathered against me; not for my transgression, nor for my sin, O Lord.

4 They run and prepare themselves without my fault: awake to help me, and behold.

5 Thou therefore, O Lord God of hosts, the God of Israel, awake to visit all the heathen: be not merciful to any wicked transgressors. Selah.

6 They return at evening: they make a noise like a dog, and go round about the city.

7 Behold, they belch out with their mouth: swords are in their lips: for who, say they, doth hear?

8 But thou, O Lord, shalt laugh at them; thou shalt have all the heathen in derision.

9 Because of his strength will I wait upon thee: for God is my defence.

10 The God of my mercy shall prevent me: God shall let me see my desire upon mine enemies.

11 Slay them not, lest my people forget: scatter them by thy power; and bring them down, O Lord our shield.

12 For the sin of their mouth and the words of their lips let them even be taken in their pride: and for cursing and lying which they speak.

13 Consume them in wrath, consume them, that they may not be: and let them know that God ruleth in Jacob unto the ends of the earth. Selah.

14 And at evening let them return; and let them make a noise like a dog, and go round about the city.

15 Let them wander up and down for meat, and grudge if they be not satisfied.

16 But I will sing of thy power; yea, I will sing aloud of thy mercy in the morning: for thou hast been my defence and refuge in the day of my trouble.

17 Unto thee, O my strength, will I sing: for God is my defence, and the God of my mercy.

For Your Information

"Workers of iniquity": evildoers.

"Bloody men": those who shed blood.

"Make a noise like a dog": howling, snarling, and growling. These are wild dogs hunting prey.

"Swords are in their lips": Their words are dangerous (see verse 12).

Psalm 59

Both a prayer and prophecy, this psalm of David follows the events in 1 Samuel 19, when jealous Saul sought to kill David because he had become Israel's most popular general. Just after the psalmist escaped, the murderers reached his home.

Following his habit, David begins with a prayer for deliverance from his enemies. Clearly God had protected him from Saul, since David's wife, Michal, who was also Saul's daughter, got wind of the king's plan. Even in these early days of his flight from Saul, David appreciated God's power over his life and the lives of his enemies.

The psalmist compares these wicked men to a pack of feral dogs, roaming the city to do evil. Dangerous hunters, they cause much damage, but God laughs at their frail power and will defend David. Eventually the evil ones will receive all the punishment David would wish on them. But he does not want them dead—like dogs whose unsuccessful hunt has left them hungry, they'll remain as an example to the people of God's powerful judgment.

David closes by rejoicing in God's power and mercy, and declaring Him as his defense.

- What limitations does God put on evil people? Can they really do all the evil they desire?

- God protected David's life, but he suffered greatly from the persecutions of Saul. Does God's protection mean that we are never hurt? What does it mean? Is there a benefit to some suffering?

Psalm 61

1 Hear my cry, O God; attend unto my prayer.

2 From the end of the earth will I cry unto thee, when my heart is overwhelmed: lead me to the rock that is higher than I.

3 For thou hast been a shelter for me, and a strong tower from the enemy.

4 I will abide in thy tabernacle for ever: I will trust in the covert of thy wings. Selah.

5 For thou, O God, hast heard my vows: thou hast given me the heritage of those that fear thy name.

6 Thou wilt prolong the king's life: and his years as many generations.

7 He shall abide before God for ever: O prepare mercy and truth, which may preserve him.

8 So will I sing praise unto thy name for ever, that I may daily perform my vows.

For Your Information

"End of the earth": symbolic of a long distance.

"The rock that is higher than I": God, who is often spoken of as a rock, to signify His unchangeable, protective nature. We are unable to reach His height in our own power.

"Covert": refuge.

"The heritage of those that fear thy name": Israel's spiritual blessings.

Psalm 61

David calls on God to listen, despite his fears that a huge distance separates them. In faith, he returns to the Redeemer, despite his recurring woes, because he has experienced God's faithfulness before, and knows he again needs His security.

Trusting that God has already heard his prayer, because David believes in Him, he believes God will bless him with long life and save him for eternity. The psalmist responds to God's grace with the praise he already vowed to Him.

- What does it mean to abide in the tabernacle (verse 4)? Can you do this during your earthly life?

- Does God always hear the prayers of His people? Could anything get in the way of His hearing? Answering?

WEEK SEVEN

Introduction

Although David faced many trials during his reign as king, they never destroyed his faith. If anything, his troubles enhanced belief, as is shown by his wonderful ability to express praise. God gave this prophet-king a heart filled with appreciation of His greatness, and the psalms that emanated from David's faith have touched believers through the ages.

David has insights into both humanity and God. The psalms speak honestly about all his trials, his desires, and failures. He is not trying to make himself look good before God when he prays. Instead he beseeches the help of his Savior. In many ways, he is a good example of how we can pray effectively. Praise as fervent as David's is rare in this world, and his trust in God, even in the face of death, shows powerful faith and understanding of his Savior.

Another frequent theme in the psalms is that of God's blessings for those who love and serve Him. In today's culture, it would be easy to attempt to use this truth to our own sinful ends and become caught up in a sort of "baptized acquisitiveness" that implies God's approval of our own selfish desires. But the generous blessings the Psalms speak of flow naturally out of faith and allow the faithful to share the truth of God's saving grace. Its naturalness has nothing to do with our desire to hoard or simply provide for our own desires. David, hiding in the wilderness, was not acquiring more material possessions, but those things essential to daily life.

The Psalms offer so much to the Christian, whether life is harsh or smooth. Because spiritual life involves all kinds of changes, the hymns of the Bible address many aspects of faith. As we read more of David's verses, which form the bulk of this week's study, we appreciate the depth of his belief and his experiences. God used his life in many ways, and through one king's praises he taught, blessed, and helped countless people.

Psalm 62

1 Truly my soul waiteth upon God: from him cometh my salvation.

2 He only is my rock and my salvation; he is my defence; I shall not be greatly moved.

3 How long will ye imagine mischief against a man? ye shall be slain all of you: as a bowing wall shall ye be, and as a tottering fence.

4 They only consult to cast him down from his excellency: they delight in lies: they bless with their mouth, but they curse inwardly. Selah.

5 My soul, wait thou only upon God; for my expectation is from him.

6 He only is my rock and my salvation: he is my defence; I shall not be moved.

7 In God is my salvation and my glory: the rock of my strength, and my refuge, is in God.

8 Trust in him at all times; ye people, pour out your heart before him: God is a refuge for us. Selah.

9 Surely men of low degree are vanity, and men of high degree are a lie: to be laid in the balance, they are altogether lighter than vanity.

10 Trust not in oppression, and become not vain in robbery: if riches increase, set not your heart upon them.

11 God hath spoken once; twice have I heard this; that power belongeth unto God.

12 Also unto thee, O Lord, belongeth mercy: for thou renderest to every man according to his work.

For Your Information

"Waiteth upon God": is silently trusting in Him.

"I shall not be greatly moved": Though he faces troubles in this world, in God, David stands firm. The end will be a good one.

"Imagine mischief": plot to cause trouble.

"Bowing wall": a weak wall, about to fall. This pictures the weakness of humanity, compared to God.

"Excellency": high place.

"Once; twice": an emphatic way of speaking. God has often shown this truth.

Psalm 62

David expresses his trust in God, his Savior, in the face of those who plot against him. Under his own power, the king cannot stand against any who seek to destroy him (verses 3–4). But David patiently waits for God to bring about his deliverance (verses 5–7) and in the following verse calls others to join him in firm faith.

Trusting in people or things is vain, but putting faith in God is not, for He judges people according to their works. David ends by calling on God to be merciful.

- When foes attacked, why didn't David simply deal with them under his own power? Was this a wise decision?

- What happens when Christians trust in people, instead of God? When they trust in things? Why do you think God has such things happen?

Psalm 63

1 O God, thou art my God; early will I seek thee: my soul thirsteth for thee, my flesh longeth for thee in a dry and thirsty land, where no water is;

2 To see thy power and thy glory, so as I have seen thee in the sanctuary.

3 Because thy lovingkindness is better than life, my lips shall praise thee.

4 Thus will I bless thee while I live: I will lift up my hands in thy name.

5 My soul shall be satisfied as with marrow and fatness; and my mouth shall praise thee with joyful lips:

6 When I remember thee upon my bed, and meditate on thee in the night watches.

7 Because thou hast been my help, therefore in the shadow of thy wings will I rejoice.

8 My soul followeth hard after thee: thy right hand upholdeth me.

9 But those that seek my soul, to destroy it, shall go into the lower parts of the earth.

10 They shall fall by the sword: they shall be a portion for foxes.

11 But the king shall rejoice in God; every one that sweareth by him shall glory: but the mouth of them that speak lies shall be stopped.

Psalm 64

1 Hear my voice, O God, in my prayer: preserve my life from fear of the enemy.

2 Hide me from the secret counsel of the wicked; from the insurrection of the workers of iniquity:

3 Who whet their tongue like a sword, and bend their bows to shoot their arrows, even bitter words:

4 That they may shoot in secret at the perfect: suddenly do they shoot at him, and fear not.

5 They encourage themselves in an evil matter: they commune of laying snares privily; they say, Who shall see them?

6 They search out iniquities; they accomplish a diligent search: both the inward thought of every one of them, and the heart, is deep.

7 But God shall shoot at them with an arrow; suddenly shall they be wounded.

8 So they shall make their own tongue to fall upon themselves: all that see them shall flee away.

9. And all men shall fear, and shall declare the work of God; for they shall wisely consider of his doing.

10 The righteous shall be glad in the Lord, and shall trust in him; and all the upright in heart shall glory.

For Your Information

"Early will I seek thee": describes the psalmist's earnest search for God.

"Thou art my God": describes David's intimate personal relationship with God.

"Dry and thirsty": a picture of the psalmist's spiritual condition.

"In thy name": to praise His perfections.

"Marrow and fatness": symbolic of good things.

"Night watches": the hours of the night.

"Shadow of thy wings": a place near God, therefore he is protected.

"The lower parts of the earth": to death.

"A portion": food.

"Privily": secretly.

"Search out": plan.

"Deep": cunning.

"Fall upon themselves": cause their own destruction.

Psalm 63

Probably written during Absalom's rebellion, this psalm of David earnestly expresses his spiritual emptiness and longing for intimate communion with God. Though in a desperate situation and uncomfortable place, the king turns to God, body and soul, and God upholds him, even in a very physically, emotionally, and spiritually difficult time.

His enemies do not have such comfort. They shall be completely destroyed, victims of their own sin. In that day, David will rejoice, along with all the faithful. But any who follow his enemies will be quelled.

• It is easy to feel spiritually empty in a negative situation. What was David's response? What were the results of his actions? What can you learn from him?

Psalm 64

Whether in the battlefield or court, David faced foes who could destroy him. Internal conspirators could end his rule as certainly as a foreign enemy, though either kind of enemy could be described here.

David seeks protection from cunning plotters and insurrectionists whose words are their weapons. Expressing confidence that God will stop their attacks and turn their own tongues against them, he remains confident this will be a testimony to God's power for all the righteous.

• Why are words so important to God? To the Christian life? What power have they had in your life?

Psalm 65

1 Praise waiteth for thee, O God, in Sion: and unto thee shall the vow be performed.

2 O thou that hearest prayer, unto thee shall all flesh come.

3 Iniquities prevail against me: as for our transgressions, thou shalt purge them away.

4 Blessed is the man whom thou choosest, and causest to approach unto thee, that he may dwell in thy courts: we shall be satisfied with the goodness of thy house, even of thy holy temple.

5 By terrible things in righteousness wilt thou answer us, O God of our salvation; who art the confidence of all the ends of the earth, and of them that are afar off upon the sea:

6 Which by his strength setteth fast the mountains; being girded with power:

7 Which stilleth the noise of the seas, the noise of their waves, and the tumult of the people.

8 They also that dwell in the uttermost parts are afraid at thy tokens: thou makest the outgoings of the morning and evening to rejoice.

9 Thou visitest the earth, and waterest it: thou greatly enrichest it with the river of God, which is full of water: thou preparest them corn, when thou hast so provided for it.

10 Thou waterest the ridges thereof abundantly: thou settlest the furrows thereof: thou makest it soft with showers: thou blessest the springing thereof.

11 Thou crownest the year with thy goodness; and thy paths drop fatness.

12 They drop upon the pastures of the wilderness: and the little hills rejoice on every side.

13 The pastures are clothed with flocks; the valleys also are covered over with corn; they shout for joy, they also sing.

For Your Information

"Sion": variant spelling for Zion, another name for Jerusalem.

"All flesh": all people.

"Dwell in thy courts": live close to God. This does not mean he lives in the temple, but has a heart close to God.

"Tokens": signs.

"River of God": a sign of God's abundance.

Psalm 65

This psalm of David, attached to no particular situation in his life, simply offers the Creator God praise for his faithfulness to his people. Though their sin overwhelmed them, God, who heard their prayers, forgave the Israelites.

The person whom God chooses is blessed with many good things, the highest of which is a relationship with Him. The natural world shows forth His glory, and the psalmist details its power in verses 5–7. The entire world sees God's wonders and fears.

David finishes by describing God's blessings upon the earth, which provide richly for his people. The world He made delights in its Creator.

• What is the Christian view of creation? How does it differ from popular views of the world today?

• God has made us stewards of His creation. What does that involve? How can it help us worship Him? What dangers do we need to avoid?

Psalm 66

1 Make a joyful noise unto God, all ye lands:

2 Sing forth the honour of his name: make his praise glorious.

3 Say unto God, How terrible art thou in thy works! through the greatness of thy power shall thine enemies submit themselves unto thee.

4 All the earth shall worship thee, and shall sing unto thee; they shall sing to thy name. Selah.

5 Come and see the works of God: he is terrible in his doing toward the children of men.

6 He turned the sea into dry land: they went through the flood on foot: there did we rejoice in him.

7 He ruleth by his power for ever; his eyes behold the nations: let not the rebellious exalt themselves. Selah.

8 O bless our God, ye people, and make the voice of his praise to be heard:

9 Which holdeth our soul in life, and suffereth not our feet to be moved.

10 For thou, O God, hast proved us: thou hast tried us, as silver is tried.

11 Thou broughtest us into the net; thou laidst affliction upon our loins.

12 Thou hast caused men to ride over our heads; we went through fire and through water: but thou broughtest us out into a wealthy place.

13 I will go into thy house with burnt offerings: I will pay thee my vows,

14 Which my lips have uttered, and my mouth hath spoken, when I was in trouble.

15 I will offer unto thee burnt sacrifices of fatlings, with the incense of rams; I will offer bullocks with goats. Selah.

16 Come and hear, all ye that fear God, and I will declare what he hath done for my soul.

17 I cried unto him with my mouth, and he was extolled with my tongue.

18 If I regard iniquity in my heart, the Lord will not hear me:

19 But verily God hath heard me; he hath attended to the voice of my prayer.

20 Blessed be God, which hath not turned away my prayer, nor his mercy from me.

For Your Information

"Make a joyful noise": shout.

"All ye lands": all nations.

"Make his praise glorious": give Him praise that tells of His glory.

"Terrible": awesome.

"Submit": They are conquered.

"Turned the sea into dry land": a reference to the Exodus (Exodus 14:21–22).

"Holdeth our soul in life": saves our souls.

"Tried": refined.

"Fatlings": fat animals.

"Ride over our heads": a description of chariots overriding fallen soldiers.

Psalm 66

This psalm invites all people to praise God and recognize the greatness of His works (verses 1–7). Some commentators see this broad call to all nations as prefiguring the coming of the Gentiles to Christ. The psalmist reminds his readers of the Exodus, when God saved the Hebrews out of Egypt (verse 6).

In response, the people praise God, who has saved them both spiritually and physically and blessed their lives with many good things (verses 8–12). The psalmist offers his own personal thanks and praises and promises to fulfill his vows to God. He tells all people of God's faithfulness and thanks Him for His answers to prayers made by those whose hearts are pure.

• Is there any person whose prayers and praises God will not hear? What is the solution to that situation?

• What wonderful things has God done for you? Have you praised Him for them? Have you shared what He has done with others?

Psalm 67

1 God be merciful unto us, and bless us; and cause his face to shine upon us; Selah.

2 That thy way may be known upon earth, thy saving health among all nations.

3 Let the people praise thee, O God; let all the people praise thee.

4 O let the nations be glad and sing for joy: for thou shalt judge the people righteously, and govern the nations upon earth. Selah.

5 Let the people praise thee, O God; let all the people praise thee.

6 Then shall the earth yield her increase; and God, even our own God, shall bless us.

7 God shall bless us; and all the ends of the earth shall fear him.

Psalm 70

1 Make haste, O God, to deliver me; make haste to help me, O Lord.

2 Let them be ashamed and confounded that seek after my soul: let them be turned backward, and put to confusion, that desire my hurt.

3 Let them be turned back for a reward of their shame that say, Aha, aha.

4 Let all those that seek thee rejoice and be glad in thee: and let such as love thy salvation say continually, Let God be magnified.

5 But I am poor and needy: make haste unto me, O God: thou art my help and my deliverer; O Lord, make no tarrying.

For Your Information

"Face to shine upon us": a picture of God's favor.

"Saving health": salvation.

"Her increase": the land's harvest. This symbolizes great spiritual blessing, too.

"Fear": be in awe.

"Aha": the mocking sounds of his enemies.

Psalm 67

Beginning in the first verse with the priestly blessing that appears in Numbers 6:24–26, this unnamed psalmist cries for God's mercy and favor. He leads the faithful in a testimony to God's salvation of His people. Not only will Israel sing His praises, but the nations will rejoice when they are ruled by God, who wields power justly. When all praise Him, abundant blessing will follow.

- When we ask for blessings from God, what kind of heart attitude do we need to have? What kind of attitudes could keep the blessing from occurring?

- If God has not blessed someone physically, does it mean that person is not blessed? Can one be physically blessed and not receive spiritual blessings? What are some different ways God blesses people?

Psalm 70

Almost identical to Psalm 40:13–17, again the psalmist exhorts God to hurry to his aid. This may have been used as an introductory psalm to Psalm 71.

Again David asks God to deliver him from enemies and frustrate their evil desires. He asks God to give them shame as a deterring reward for their wickedness. Yet all those who love God will rejoice at His defense of the psalmist, because they share in God's salvation. In the last verse, David again speaks personally, describing his great need for God's help and deliverance to come quickly.

- Is anyone beyond needing God's assistance in life? Why do you think that is so? Is it wrong for David to want God to turn back his enemies? Why or why not?

- When God does not come with assistance quickly, is it because He does not care? Can God ever respond too late?

Psalm 71

1 In thee, O Lord, do I put my trust: let me never be put to confusion.

2 Deliver me in thy righteousness, and cause me to escape: incline thine ear unto me, and save me.

3 Be thou my strong habitation, whereunto I may continually resort: thou hast given commandment to save me; for thou art my rock and my fortress.

4 Deliver me, O my God, out of the hand of the wicked, out of the hand of the unrighteous and cruel man.

5 For thou art my hope, O Lord God: thou art my trust from my youth.

6 By thee have I been holden up from the womb: thou art he that took me out of my mother's bowels: my praise shall be continually of thee.

7 I am as a wonder unto many; but thou art my strong refuge.

8 Let my mouth be filled with thy praise and with thy honour all the day.

9 Cast me not off in the time of old age; forsake me not when my strength faileth.

10 For mine enemies speak against me; and they that lay wait for my soul take counsel together,

11 Saying, God hath forsaken him: persecute and take him; for there is none to deliver him.

12 O God, be not far from me: O my God, make haste for my help.

13 Let them be confounded and consumed that are adversaries to my soul; let them be covered with reproach and dishonour that seek my hurt.

14 But I will hope continually, and will yet praise thee more and more.

15 My mouth shall shew forth thy righteousness and thy salvation all the day; for I know not the numbers thereof.

16 I will go in the strength of the Lord God: I will make mention of thy righteousness, even of thine only.

17 O God, thou hast taught me from my youth: and hitherto have I declared thy wondrous works.

18 Now also when I am old and grayheaded, O God, forsake me not; until I have shewed thy strength unto this generation, and thy

power to every one that is to come.

19 Thy righteousness also, O God, is very high, who hast done great things: O God, who is like unto thee!

20 Thou, which hast shewed me great and sore troubles, shalt quicken me again, and shalt bring me up again from the depths of the earth.

21 Thou shalt increase my greatness, and comfort me on every side.

22 I will also praise thee with the psaltery, even thy truth, O my God: unto thee will I sing with the harp, O thou Holy one of Israel.

23 My lips shall greatly rejoice when I sing unto thee; and my soul, which thou hast redeemed.

24 My tongue also shall talk of thy righteousness all the day long: for they are confounded, for they are brought unto shame, that seek my hurt.

For Your Information

"Given commandment": ordained.

"Holden": held.

"Bowels": inner parts.

"I will go in the strength": According to Charles H. Spurgeon, it is better translated "I will come with the mighty deeds." The psalmist declares God's greatness.

"Sore": extreme.

Psalm 71

Possibly used with the previous psalm as an introduction and quite probably written by David, these verses declare the habitual reliance of the psalmist on God. The thread of his intense need for God runs through the psalm, alternating with examples of his trust in his Lord. God has supported the psalmist from the time of his birth, and his praises for the One who saved him continue. He has become a testimony to others, because of his faithfulness.

But his past faithfulness has not lessened his need for God's aid. As an old man, he relies on God at least as much as in his youth, and he still wants to testify to all of his Lord's faithfulness. The psalmist praises God's righteousness and faithfulness and continues to laud the God who has never deserted him.

• Name some ways in which it is implied God had been faithful to the psalmist. Has He been faithful to you in some of these ways, too?

• Does God forsake people simply because they become old? What reasons did the psalmist have to believe God would remain faithful?

Psalm 72

1 Give the king thy judgments, O God, and thy righteousness unto the king's son.

2 He shall judge thy people with righteousness, and thy poor with judgment.

3 The mountains shall bring peace to the people, and the little hills, by righteousness.

4 He shall judge the poor of the people, he shall save the children of the needy, and shall break in pieces the oppressor.

5 They shall fear thee as long as the sun and moon endure, throughout all generations.

6 He shall come down like rain upon the mown grass: as showers that water the earth.

7 In his days shall the righteous flourish; and abundance of peace so long as the moon endureth.

8 He shall have dominion also from sea to sea, and from the river unto the ends of the earth.

9 They that dwell in the wilderness shall bow before him; and his enemies shall lick the dust.

10 The kings of Tarshish and of the isles shall bring presents: the kings of Sheba and Seba shall offer gifts.

11 Yea, all kings shall fall down before him: all nations shall serve him.

12 For he shall deliver the needy when he crieth; the poor also, and him that hath no helper.

13 He shall spare the poor and needy, and shall save the souls of the needy.

14 He shall redeem their soul from deceit and violence: and precious shall their blood be in his sight.

15 And he shall live, and to him shall be given of the gold of Sheba: prayer also shall be made for him continually; and daily shall he be praised.

16 There shall be an handful of corn in the earth upon the top of the mountains; the fruit thereof shall shake like Lebanon: and they of the city shall flourish like grass of the earth.

17 His name shall endure for ever: his name shall be continued as long as the sun: and men shall be blessed in him: all nations shall call him blessed.

18 Blessed be the Lord God, the God of Israel, who only doeth wondrous things.

19 And blessed be his glorious name for ever: and let the whole earth be filled with his glory; Amen, and Amen.

20 The prayers of David the son of Jesse are ended.

For Your Information

"Judgments": rule based on God's wisdom.

"King's son": another name for the king.

"Sheba": a mountainous country in southwest Arabia.

"Seba": an area of uncertain location, possibly in Cush (modern-day Sudan) or elsewhere in East Africa.

Psalm 72

The bulk of the psalms of David end here (see verse 20), with a prayer for his son Solomon, whom David had anointed king before his own death (1 Kings 1:28–40). Indeed, in a historical sense this psalm ends David's story, as he passes on the throne. But this is also more than a song for Solomon. It is a Messianic psalm, as it prefigures Jesus' rule as King of all the earth. The powers spoken of in verse 3–17 are obviously beyond those of even the most powerful king. But a righteous earthly king should attempt to create the justice described here and should care for his people, encouraging abundance in the land. The verses end with a description of the blessings of the king's reign.

Verses 18–19 are a doxology, ending the second book of the Psalms. They lift up God's glory, which fills the earth.

- What ideas of a righteous government are outlined here? What would its basis be? How does it compare to present-day governments?

- What picture do you get of Jesus here? What parts have been fulfilled? What will be fulfilled when He comes in glory?

WEEK EIGHT

Introduction

This week we cover Book 3 of the Psalms, a short grouping. Because space does not allow all the chapters to be included here, I have chosen among them, considering content and length. Readers may also wish to study the psalms not included here, because they should understand much of them, based on what we have already considered. Many of the ideas and themes of the psalms already discussed will appear in them, and it can be a good opportunity for students to discover how much they have retained.

As David's psalms are only represented by Psalm 86, there are new names associated with these verses. Asaph, the author of Psalms 73–83, was a priest in David's era who, along with his sons, led music in the temple worship. Though some have questioned whether Asaph wrote them or they were dedicated to him, 2 Chronicles 29:30 and the linking of his name with David's would seem to indicate the former.

Psalms 84–88 are dedicated to the sons of Korah, who were singers in the temple (2 Chronicles 20:19). Altogether, eleven psalms in the book of Psalms were written for them.

Following David's death, his son Solomon reigned. But after Solomon's death, the kingdom split into two parts, Israel, which consisted of the ten tribes in the north, and Judah, made up of the two southern tribes. This is a time of much warfare and turmoil. The political division lasted until after the Babylonians attacked and overthrew first Israel and then Judah.

Spiritual turmoil predated and accompanied the national upheaval. Solomon had married many foreign wives, and paganism began to influence the entire culture. Few people followed God faithfully, and Israel was hardly at the height of its spiritual influence. The troubles faced by the nation are also reflected by the psalmists, who saw the connection between the experiences of their nation and the hand of God. He judged their wrongdoing, and the entire nation needed to seek forgiveness and walk in a new path.

But where humanity was not faithful, God was. He restored the Jews to their land after the Persian Cyrus the Great conquered Babylon. Cyrus reversed the earlier policies in 539 B.C., reversing the deportation of conquered peoples, and some Jews returned to Israel. But their once flourishing country was much debased. Jerusalem required extensive rebuilding, as described by Nehemiah and Ezra in the books that bear their names. But the Israelites did rebuild. Despite their sin, God had not deserted them, and Israel left behind the paganism that had separated them.

Psalm 73

1 Truly God is good to Israel, even to such as are of a clean heart.

2 But as for me. . .my steps had well nigh slipped.

3 For I was envious. . .when I saw the prosperity of the wicked.

4 For there are no bands in their death: but their strength is firm.

5 They are not in trouble as other men. . . .

6 Therefore pride compasseth them about. . .violence covereth them as a garment.

7 . . .They have more than heart could wish.

8 They are corrupt. . . .

9 They set their mouth against the heavens. . . .

10 Therefore his people return hither: and waters of a full cup are wrung out to them.

11 And they say, How doth God know? . . .

12 Behold, these are the ungodly, who prosper in the world. . . .

13 I have cleansed my heart in vain. . . .

14 For all the day long have I been plagued. . . .

16 It was too painful for me;

17 Until I went into the sanctuary of God; then understood I their end.

18 Surely thou didst set them in slippery places. . . .

19 How are they brought into desolation, as in a moment! . . .

20 . . .Thou shalt despise their image.

21 Thus my heart was grieved. . . .

22 So foolish was I, and ignorant: I was as a beast before thee.

23 Nevertheless I am continually with thee: thou hast holden me by my right hand.

24 Thou shalt guide me with thy counsel, and afterward receive me to glory.

25 Whom have I in heaven but thee? and there is none upon earth that I desire beside thee.

26 My flesh and my heart faileth: but God is the strength of my heart, and my portion for ever.

27 For, lo, they that are far from thee shall perish. . . .

28 But. . .I have put my trust in the Lord God, that I may declare all thy works.

Psalm 75

1 Unto thee, O God, do we give thanks. . .for that thy name is near thy wondrous works declare.

2 When I shall receive the congregation I will judge uprightly.

3 The earth and all the inhabitants thereof are dissolved: I bear up the pillars of it. Selah.

4 I said unto the fools, Deal not foolishly: and to the wicked, Lift not up the horn:

5 . . .Speak not with a stiff neck.

6 For promotion cometh neither from the east, nor from the west, nor from the south.

7 But God is the judge: he putteth down one, and setteth up another.

8 For in the hand of the Lord there is a cup, and the wine is red; it is full of mixture; and he poureth out of the same: but the dregs thereof, all the wicked of the earth shall wring them out, and drink them.

9 But I will. . .sing praises to the God of Jacob.

10 All the horns of the wicked also will I cut off; but the horns of the righteous shall be exalted.

For Your Information

"Israel": those who trust in God.

"Clean heart": one whose heart is pure before God.

"Bands": pangs.

"Set their mouth against the heavens": They blaspheme against God.

"Wrung out to them": They drink from a bitter cup.

"Slippery places": a precarious position.

"Portion": Inheritance.

"Thy name is near": His perfections and protection are at hand.

"Receive the congregation": choose the proper time.

"Pillars": the earth's supports.

"Horn": usually symbolizes either honor or strength. Here it symbolizes defiance.

"Promotion": exaltation.

"The wine is red": symbolizes wrath.

Psalm 73

Asaph's first psalm in the psalter compares the rewards of the wicked and the godly. Why, we often ask, don't the wicked seem to get their just deserts? He provides us with the answer here.

The psalmist began to doubt when he saw the wicked doing so well in this world. Despite their attitude towards God, they received many physical blessings. So the psalmist began to question the value of godliness—until he went to the Temple and considered the end of those who denied God. The Lord has put the wicked in a dangerous place. Though they do not see the judgment ahead of them, they will be utterly destroyed.

The psalmist repents of his doubts and instead delights in his eternal future with God.

- Why does God allow the wicked many possessions on earth? What possession are they missing? Which is more important?

Psalm 75

Another of Asaph's psalms begins with thanksgiving for God's perfect character. In response to this praise, God speaks in verses 2–5 and promises He will judge rightly and give the wicked their due. Their opposition comes to nothing, for compared to God, they are frail. Only He can exalt a man or put him down. He shows His wrath against the wicked.

But the psalmist praises God for his judgment, for He exalts His people.

- How does God bring down the wicked? Exalt His people? What if we do not see these judgments during our lifetimes?

Psalm 76

1 In Judah is God known: his name is great in Israel.

2 In Salem also is his tabernacle, and his dwelling place in Zion.

3 There brake he the arrows of the bow, the shield, and the sword, and the battle. Selah.

4 Thou art more glorious and excellent than the mountains of prey.

5 The stouthearted are spoiled, they have slept their sleep: and none of the men of might have found their hands.

6 At thy rebuke, O God of Jacob, both the chariot and horse are cast into a dead sleep.

7 Thou, even thou, art to be feared: and who may stand in thy sight when once thou art angry?

8 Thou didst cause judgment to be heard from heaven; the earth feared, and was still,

9 When God arose to judgment, to save all the meek of the earth. Selah.

10 Surely the wrath of man shall praise thee: the remainder of wrath shalt thou restrain.

11 Vow, and pay unto the Lord your God: let all that be round about him bring presents unto him that ought to be feared.

12 He shall cut off the spirit of princes: he is terrible to the kings of the earth.

Psalm 77

1 I cried unto God with my voice. . .and he gave ear unto me.

2 In the day of my trouble I sought the Lord. . .my soul refused to be comforted.

3 I remembered God, and was troubled. . . .

4 Thou holdest mine eyes waking: I am so troubled that I cannot speak.

5 I have considered the days of old. . . .

6 I call to remembrance my song in the night: I commune with mine own heart: and my spirit made diligent search.

7 Will the Lord cast off for ever? and will he be favourable no more? . . .

9 Hath God forgotten to be gracious? hath he in anger shut up his tender mercies? Selah.

10 And I said, This is my infirmity: but I will remember the years of the right hand of the most High.

11 I will remember the works of the Lord. . . .

12 I will meditate also of all thy work, and talk of thy doings.

13 Thy way, O God, is in the sanctuary: who is so great a God as our God?

14 Thou art the God that doest wonders: thou hast declared thy strength among the people.

15 Thou hast with thine arm redeemed thy people, the sons of Jacob and Joseph. Selah.

16 The waters saw thee, O God, the waters saw thee; they were afraid: the depths also were troubled.

17 The clouds poured out water: the skies sent out a sound: thine arrows also went abroad.

18 The voice of thy thunder was in the heaven. . .the earth trembled and shook.

19 Thy way is in the sea. . .and thy footsteps are not known.

20 Thou leddest thy people like a flock by the hand of Moses and Aaron.

For Your Information

"Judah. . .Israel": both people of God's covenant.

"Salem": Jerusalem.

"Mountains of prey": The lairs of lions in the mountains are compared to the invading power.

"Are spoiled": they fear.

"Slept their sleep": the sleep of death.

"None. . .found their hands": They are powerless.

"Wrath of man": When men rise against God, He crushes them, showing His own glory.

"Cut off the spirit of princes": destroys their leaders.

"Is terrible to": is feared by.

"Gave ear unto": heard.

"Holdest mine eyes waking": keep me awake.

"Shut up": stopped.

"Years of the right hand": God's power has given him this test, but it can also change things.

"Jacob and Joseph": all the Jews.

"The waters saw thee": a reference to the Red Sea and the Exodus.

Psalm 76
Asaph's psalm commemorates the overthrow of the Assyrians attacking Israel (see 2 Kings 19:31). God is known for His power, as He has overthrown the enemy. The psalmist praises Him for the destruction of the Jews' enemy through His powerful judgments and ends by encouraging those who believe to be faithful to Him and honor their God.

• Read the amazing story of God's salvation of the Jews from the Assyrian power. Can you name some other places in the psalms where a psalmist tells of a historical salvation? Does this encourage you to trust that He will help you?

Psalm 77
Again Asaph cries out to God when he is distressed and needs comfort, and God hears. Asaph describes his very personal anguish and fears (verses 3–9). Then his thoughts turn to a solution, as he remembers and meditates on God's works and praises Him for His providence (verses 10–20). Pondering God's wonders and all He has done for His people, he poetically describes the Exodus as the God of creation protected them from their enemy.

• Has God been faithful for you? How? As you think of His past faithfulness, are you encouraged for your current faith challenges?

Psalm 80

1 Give ear, O Shepherd of Israel, thou that leadest Joseph like a flock; thou that dwellest between the cherubims, shine forth.

2 Before Ephraim and Benjamin and Manasseh stir up thy strength, and come and save us.

3 Turn us again, O God, and cause thy face to shine; and we shall be saved.

4 O Lord God of hosts, how long wilt thou be angry against the prayer of thy people?

5 Thou feedest them with the bread of tears; and givest them tears to drink in great measure.

6 Thou makest us a strife unto our neighbours: and our enemies laugh among themselves.

7 Turn us again, O God of hosts, and cause thy face to shine; and we shall be saved.

8 Thou hast brought a vine out of Egypt: thou hast cast out the heathen, and planted it.

9 Thou preparedst room before it, and didst cause it to take deep root, and it filled the land.

10 The hills were covered with the shadow of it, and the boughs thereof were like the goodly cedars.

11 She sent out her boughs unto the sea, and her branches unto the river.

12 Why hast thou then broken down her hedges, so that all they which pass by the way do pluck her?

13 The boar out of the wood doth waste it, and the wild beast of the field doth devour it.

14 Return, we beseech thee, O God of hosts: look down from heaven, and behold, and visit this vine;

15 And the vineyard which thy right hand hath planted, and the branch that thou madest strong for thyself.

16 It is burned with fire, it is cut down: they perish at the rebuke of thy countenance.

17 Let thy hand be upon the man of thy right hand, upon the son of man whom thou madest strong for thyself.

18 So will not we go back from thee: quicken us, and we will call upon thy name.

19 Turn us again, O Lord God of hosts, cause thy face to shine; and we shall be saved.

Psalm 82

1 God standeth in the congregation of the mighty; he judgeth among the gods.

2 How long will ye judge unjustly, and accept the persons of the wicked? Selah.

3 Defend the poor and fatherless: do justice to the afflicted and needy.

4 Deliver the poor and needy: rid them out of the hand of the wicked.

5 They know not, neither will they understand; they walk on in darkness: all the foundations of the earth are out of course.

6 I have said, Ye are gods; and all of you are children of the most High.

7 But ye shall die like men, and fall like one of the princes.

8 Arise, O God, judge the earth: for thou shalt inherit all nations.

For Your Information

"Shepherd": God leads the flock of His people.

"Dwellest between the cherubims": God's presence was revealed on the mercy seat, the lid of the ark, which lay between two cherubim.

"Joseph. . . Ephraim and Benjamin and Manasseh": Israel had split into two nations, Israel and Judah. This probably symbolizes the northern kingdom, Israel.

"Thy face to shine": a sign of God's favor.

"Bread of tears": symbolic of affliction.

"Goodly cedars": a picture of God's might.

"Hedges": surrounding and protecting the vineyard.

"Boar. . .wild beast": symbolizes the attacking heathen nations.

"The man of thy right hand": Benjamin, whose name means "son of my right hand." This is a Messianic prophecy.

"The mighty": rulers and judges.

"Gods": an honorific title given to Near Eastern rulers and judges, ruling in their "gods" names.

"Accept the persons": show partiality.

Psalm 80

Asaph calls on God to hear and save His people and seeks to end His anger and gain His favor. He reminds God He rescued the people from slavery in Egypt and planted them in Israel. Like a grapevine, they spread into the Promised Land. Abandoned, they are prey to enemies. He calls on God to send a man with His power. Then God's Spirit will quicken their spirits and save Israel.

• When Asaph wrote this psalm, had God deserted His people? What had happened? (See verse 19 for a hint.) Did God give them His favor again?

Psalm 82

In this psalm of Asaph, God judges rulers and judges. These immoral men have judged wickedly, instead of ruling honestly and wisely. So God will judge them, and they shall die. The psalmist asks God to bring justice to the earth quickly.

• Is anyone above God's justice? Does it always seem that way? Can you trust God to bring justice?

Psalm 81

1 Sing aloud unto God our strength: make a joyful noise unto the God of Jacob.

2 Take a psalm, and bring hither the timbrel, the pleasant harp with the psaltery.

3 Blow up the trumpet in the new moon, in the time appointed, on our solemn feast day.

4 For this was a statute for Israel, and a law of the God of Jacob.

5 This he ordained in Joseph for a testimony, when he went out through the land of Egypt: where I heard a language that I understood not.

6 I removed his shoulder from the burden: his hands were delivered from the pots.

7 Thou calledst in trouble, and I delivered thee; I answered thee in the secret place of thunder: I proved thee at the waters of Meribah. Selah.

8 Hear, O my people, and I will testify unto thee: O Israel, if thou wilt hearken unto me;

9 There shall no strange god be in thee; neither shalt thou worship any strange god.

10 I am the Lord thy God, which brought thee out of the land of Egypt: open thy mouth wide, and I will fill it.

11 But my people would not hearken to my voice; and Israel would none of me.

12 So I gave them up unto their own hearts' lust: and they walked in their own counsels.

13 Oh that my people had hearkened unto me, and Israel had walked in my ways!

14 I should soon have subdued their enemies, and turned my hand against their adversaries.

15 The haters of the Lord should have submitted themselves unto him: but their time should have endured for ever.

16 He should have fed them also with the finest of the wheat: and with honey out of the rock should I have satisfied thee.

Psalm 87

1 His foundation is in the holy mountains.

2 The Lord loveth the gates of Zion more than all the dwellings of Jacob.

3 Glorious things are spoken of thee, O city of God. Selah.

4 I will make mention of Rahab and Babylon to them that know me: behold Philistia, and Tyre, with Ethiopia; this man was born there.

5 And of Zion it shall be said, This and that man was born in her: and the highest himself shall establish her.

6 The Lord shall count, when he writeth up the people, that this man was born there. Selah.

7 As well the singers as the players on instruments shall be there: all my springs are in thee.

For Your Information

"A joyful noise": shout.

"Timbrel": tambourine.

"Blow up the trumpet": sound the ram's horn trumpet (shofar).

"New moon": month.

"Removed his shoulder from the burden. . .the pots": delivered Israel from slavery in Egypt.

"Meribah": a place of testing where Israel grumbled against God (Exodus 17:1–7).

"Secret place of thunder": the pillar of fire (Exodus 14, 15).

"Honey out of the rock": In the Promised Land, bees sometimes built their hives in rocky places.

"Rahab": Egypt (see Isaiah 30:7).

"Babylon. . .Philistia. . .Tyre. . .Ethiopia": Gentile nations.

"Springs": an obscure term that may signify joy or refreshment.

Psalm 81

Asaph wrote this psalm for a festival, though commentators disagree about which one. He calls on believers to loudly praise God, using many instruments, including a ram's horn trumpet as God commanded in Leviticus 23:24 for the New Year celebration.

God delivered them from slavery in Egypt and, though they grumbled, provided water in the desert. But they still turned from Him. So He sorrowfully gave them over to their sin. Verses 13–16 outline the blessings He would have offered them, had they obeyed.

- Is worship always supposed to be "proper"? In what way? Are shouts an appropriate way to praise God?

Psalm 87

This prophetic praise psalm for the sons of Korah celebrates the city of Jerusalem, where God founded His city and temple. It alone of all the psalms draws a picture of the Gentile nations coming to God to be treated as native believers. One day, they shall worship in Jerusalem, and find joy in God.

- Does God equally accept both Jews and Gentiles who love Him? Do you have that same ability?

Psalm 83

1 Keep not thou silence, O God: hold not thy peace, and be not still, O God.

2 For, lo, thine enemies make a tumult: and they that hate thee have lifted up the head.

3 They have taken crafty counsel against thy people, and consulted against thy hidden ones.

4 They have said, Come, and let us cut them off from being a nation; that the name of Israel may be no more in remembrance.

5 For they have consulted together with one consent: they are confederate against thee:

6 The tabernacles of Edom, and the Ishmaelites; of Moab, and the Hagarenes;

7 Gebal, and Ammon, and Amalek; the Philistines with the inhabitants of Tyre;

8 Assur also is joined with them: they have holpen the children of lot. Selah.

9 Do unto them as unto the Midianites; as to Sisera, as to Jabin, at the brook of Kison:

10 Which perished at Endor: they became as dung for the earth.

11 Make their nobles like Oreb, and like Zeeb: yea, all their princes as Zebah, and as Zalmunna:

12 Who said, Let us take to ourselves the houses of God in possession.

13 O my God, make them like a wheel; as the stubble before the wind.

14 As the fire burneth a wood, and as the flame setteth the mountains on fire;

15 So persecute them with thy tempest, and make them afraid with thy storm.

16 Fill their faces with shame; that they may seek thy name, O Lord.

17 Let them be confounded and troubled for ever; yea, let them be put to shame, and perish:

18 That men may know that thou, whose name alone is Jehovah, art the most high over all the earth.

For Your Information

"Lifted up the head": a sign of pride against God.

"Hidden ones": those whom God protects, His people.

"Edom. . .the children of Lot": a listing of the enemies of Israel. Though no historic event shows this collection of allies, it may refer to the events in 2 Chronicles 20.

"Holpen": helped.

"Midianites. . .Kison": refers to victories over Israel's enemies in the times of the Judges (see Judges 7, 4).

"Endor": a place where many fleeing soldiers were slain.

"Oreb and Zalmunna": Midianite leaders.

"Houses": flock enclosures.

"A wheel": a light, whirling thing.

"Jehovah": a corruption of the name *Yahweh*, which means "the Lord." The psalmist is praising God's power and authority, which the enemies have bowed to.

Psalm 83

Asaph calls on God not to withhold His help from His people Israel as a confederation of enemies attack. Israel's enemies have conspired to assault and destroy her.

The psalmist outlines the enemies, each of which have previously been overcome by God's power. But they have not learned. They still come against His people, thinking they will wipe them off the face of the earth. These adversaries have invaded the place where God keeps His people safe.

Asaph asks God to take away their strength and persecute them with His creation. *May they experience shame and destruction*, he asks, *so that people will know You are Lord.*

- Did the enemies have a real chance of wiping out Israel? Why or why not? Why do you think they attacked again, even though they'd been previously defeated? Was this a spiritual or logical choice?

- What does it mean to have God as Lord? What change would this make in the nations?

Psalm 84

1 How amiable are thy tabernacles, O Lord of hosts!

2 My soul longeth, yea, even fainteth for the courts of the Lord: my heart and my flesh crieth out for the living God.

3 Yea, the sparrow hath found an house, and the swallow a nest for herself, where she may lay her young, even thine altars, O Lord of hosts, my King, and my God.

4 Blessed are they that dwell in thy house: they will be still praising thee. Selah.

5 Blessed is the man whose strength is in thee; in whose heart are the ways of them.

6 Who passing through the valley of Baca make it a well; the rain also filleth the pools.

7 They go from strength to strength, every one of them in Zion appeareth before God.

8 O Lord God of hosts, hear my prayer: give ear, O God of Jacob. Selah.

9 Behold, O God our shield, and look upon the face of thine anointed.

10 For a day in thy courts is better than a thousand. I had rather be a doorkeeper in the house of my God, than to dwell in the tents of wickedness.

11 For the Lord God is a sun and shield: the Lord will give grace and glory: no good thing will he withhold from them that walk uprightly.

12 O Lord of hosts, blessed is the man that trusteth in thee.

Psalm 85

1 Lord, thou hast been favourable unto thy land: thou hast brought back the captivity of Jacob.

2 Thou hast forgiven the iniquity of thy people, thou hast covered all their sin. Selah.

3 Thou hast taken away all thy wrath: thou hast turned thyself from the fierceness of thine anger.

4 Turn us, O God of our salvation, and cause thine anger toward us to cease.

5 Wilt thou be angry with us for ever? wilt thou draw out thine anger to all generations?

6 Wilt thou not revive us again: that thy people may rejoice in thee?

7 Shew us thy mercy, O Lord, and grant us thy salvation.

8 I will hear what God the Lord will speak: for he will speak peace unto his people, and to his saints: but let them not turn again to folly.

9 Surely his salvation is nigh them that fear him; that glory may dwell in our land.

10 Mercy and truth are met together; righteousness and peace have kissed each other.

11 Truth shall spring out of the earth; and righteousness shall look down from heaven.

12 Yea, the Lord shall give that which is good; and our land shall yield her increase.

13 Righteousness shall go before him; and shall set us in the way of his steps.

For Your Information

"Amiable": beloved.

"Tabernacles": plural because it was set up in so many places or because it had numerous courts.

"Courts": of the temple.

"In whose heart are the ways of them": whose heart wants to follow in God's ways.

"Passing": on the way to the temple.

"Valley of Baca": *Baca* may mean "weeping." An arid place, physically and spiritually.

"Pools": symbolize physical and spiritual refreshment.

"Doorkeeper": a position of humble service to God.

"Anointed": the line of David or Jesus.

"Brought back the captivity": the Jews' return from the Babylonian captivity.

Psalm 84

An unknown psalmist longs desperately to worship in the temple and feels less fortunate than the sparrows who nested near God's altar. Verses 5–7 picture the blessed worshipers heading for the temple, refreshed by God's Spirit.

The psalmist calls on God to show favor. He desires a lowly place in the temple rather than life with the wicked. He ends with praise for God's blessing on His people.

• Why is closeness with God better than the delights of the wicked? What keeps us from enjoying His nearness?

Psalm 85

An unnamed psalmist begins by remembering days of God's favor, when He forgave Israel. But sin caused a rift between God and His people, who need to repent. The psalmist calls on God to end His anger and bring them spiritual revival.

He trusts God will do this for those who seek Him but warns believers not to turn to folly again. For those who reverence Him, God pours out the blessings described in verses 10–11 on his people. Even their land will benefit. But His people must prepare for Him, seeking righteousness.

• Why does God let sinners feel His anger? Does He delight in this? In saving those who believe? How do you know?

Psalm 88

1 O Lord God of my salvation, I have cried day and night before thee:

2 Let my prayer come before thee: incline thine ear unto my cry;

3 For my soul is full of troubles: and my life draweth nigh unto the grave.

4 I am counted with them that go down into the pit: I am as a man that hath no strength:

5 Free among the dead, like the slain that lie in the grave, whom thou rememberest no more: and they are cut off from thy hand.

6 Thou hast laid me in the lowest pit, in darkness, in the deeps.

7 Thy wrath lieth hard upon me, and thou hast afflicted me with all thy waves. Selah.

8 Thou hast put away mine acquaintance far from me; thou hast made me an abomination unto them: I am shut up, and I cannot come forth.

9 Mine eye mourneth by reason of affliction: Lord, I have called daily upon thee, I have stretched out my hands unto thee.

10 Wilt thou shew wonders to the dead? shall the dead arise and praise thee? Selah.

11 Shall thy lovingkindness be declared in the grave? or thy faithfulness in destruction?

12 Shall thy wonders be known in the dark? and thy righteousness in the land of forgetfulness?

13 But unto thee have I cried, O Lord; and in the morning shall my prayer prevent thee.

14 Lord, why castest thou off my soul? why hidest thou thy face from me?

15 I am afflicted and ready to die from my youth up: while I suffer thy terrors I am distracted.

16 Thy fierce wrath goeth over me; thy terrors have cut me off.

17 They came round about me daily like water; they compassed me about together.

18 Lover and friend hast thou put far from me, and mine acquaintance into darkness.

For Your Information
"Grave": death.

"Cut off from thy hand": separated from God's earthly care.

Psalm 88

This mournful psalm has no praise after the first verse, which calls on God for salvation. Like many Christians, the psalmist has not had an easy life. He is troubled spiritually and physically, and fears he faces death. To him death appears not as a victorious reunion with God, but a separation and a senseless thing, since those in death cannot show forth God's faithfulness on earth.

He is separated by his trouble from all who know and love him (see verses 8, 18). In his loneliness, the psalmist still calls out to God. Not understanding the purpose of his suffering, he asks God what value it has (verses 10–12). He reminds God that he has not stopped praying but wonders why God has not responded. Though he has been ready to face God since his youth, he sees terrors that distract him from his spiritual purpose. He feels cut off, even from God.

Despite all his doubts and worries, the psalmist has not denied his Savior. Though the psalm ends without a solution to his problem, he has not deserted his faith.

• Do all people who suffer receive a simple response from God about the reasons for their pain? Can we assume anything about those who do not get a quick answer about their experiences?

• What does it mean when God is your salvation? Does He save in different ways? Was God still the psalmist's salvation? What signs of it can you see in this psalm?

WEEK NINE

Introduction

Again, in one week we will cover one book of the Psalms. Many are orphan psalms: Psalms 91, 93–97, 99. The works of these unidentified writers appear grouped together here and in Book 5.

Psalms 93–99 are royal praise psalms that glorify God as a magnificent king and display the believer's role as obedient subject. In various ways, the psalmists show the Lord as a powerful Near Eastern ruler showing forth His authority. The descriptions are not familiar to us, yet they leave us with a sense of awe uncommon in our democratic experience. But no matter what form of government we rely on, scripture's message is always clear: God rules the earth, including people, and we are to look to Him as we make all our decisions and obey Him consistently.

God's protection is also a common theme in the Psalms. Whereas He creates all beings and calls them to love and obey Him, not all respond to that invitation. So when the Psalms speak of His protection, recognize that it does not cover everyone. Those who reject Him have chosen their own path instead of God's and remain protectionless; that is the price of disobedience. But those who serve God are under His authority and care, and He watches over them, often using His great authority to keep them safe. So the immense power shown by God in the verses that picture Him as an omnipotent ruler may awe the believer, but need not cause terror. His anger may fall on those who trust in Him, but only when sin separates them from Him. Even when a Christian falls away, God will woo the loved one back, at least for a time. Stern anger only follows intense disobedience.

The proper response to the awesome view of God we see so often in these psalms are adoration and obedience. When we know the strength of the Lord we serve and have felt His intense love for us, our hearts and spirits should be humbled. For the Psalms are not simply verses of pretty poetry, they are meant to impact our lives and change our hearts. When they do that, we are relating to scripture the way God intended us to.

Psalm 90

1 Lord, thou hast been our dwelling place in all generations.

2 Before the mountains were brought forth, or ever thou hadst formed the earth and the world, even from everlasting to everlasting, thou art God.

3 Thou turnest man to destruction; and sayest, Return, ye children of men.

4 For a thousand years in thy sight are but as yesterday when it is past, and as a watch in the night.

5 Thou carriest them away as with a flood; they are as a sleep: in the morning they are like grass which groweth up.

6 In the morning it flourisheth, and groweth up; in the evening it is cut down, and withereth.

7 For we are consumed by thine anger, and by thy wrath are we troubled.

8 Thou hast set our iniquities before thee, our secret sins in the light of thy countenance.

9 For all our days are passed away in thy wrath: we spend our years as a tale that is told.

10 The days of our years are threescore years and ten; and if by reason of strength they be fourscore years, yet is their strength labour and sorrow; for it is soon cut off, and we fly away.

11 Who knoweth the power of thine anger? even according to thy fear, so is thy wrath.

12 So teach us to number our days, that we may apply our hearts unto wisdom.

13 Return, O Lord, how long? and let it repent thee concerning thy servants.

14 O satisfy us early with thy mercy; that we may rejoice and be glad all our days.

15 Make us glad according to the days wherein thou hast afflicted us, and the years wherein we have seen evil.

16 Let thy work appear unto thy servants, and thy glory unto their children.

17 And let the beauty of the Lord our God be upon us: and establish thou the work of our hands upon us; yea, the work of our hands establish thou it.

Psalm 93

1 The Lord reigneth, he is clothed with majesty; the Lord is clothed with strength, wherewith he hath girded himself: the world also is stablished, that it cannot be moved.

2 Thy throne is established of old: thou art from everlasting.

3 The floods have lifted up, O Lord, the floods have lifted up their voice; the floods lift up their waves.

4 The Lord on high is mightier than the noise of many waters, yea, than the mighty waves of the sea.

5 Thy testimonies are very sure: holiness becometh thine house, O Lord, for ever.

For Your Information

"Dwelling place": home, refuge.

"Turnest man to destruction": ends mankind's physical life.

"Return": to God, in repentance.

"Watch": a turn on guard duty, a third of the night.

"Carriest them away as with a flood": their years flow by swiftly.

"A tale that is told": as brief as the spoken word.

"Threescore and ten": seventy. A score is twenty.

"Early": in youth.

"Girded": armed.

"Stablished": established.

"Floods": early creation's untamed waters.

"Testimonies": His divine truth.

Psalm 90

Moses' psalm was probably written sometime after the Exodus. The prophet is keenly aware of the sinfulness of people, compared to the holiness of the God who, from very creation, has been their protection.

He makes the reader aware of human sinfulness and frailty (verses 1–6), describes the just judgment God makes for sin (verses 7–12), and asks for God's mercy upon His people (verses 13–17).

• Moses reminds us to number our days. How can we do that? What differences will it make in our lives?

Psalm 93

An orphan psalm begins a series of royal psalms (Psalms 93–100) that celebrate God's reign. This one declares God's authority over the earth, which He has wielded from all eternity. Creation itself declares God's power, as the newly made seas rush forth, but their awesome strength pales beside the Lord whose greatness they declare. The psalmist ends by declaring the unchangeableness of God's truths and His endless holiness.

• God's authority in creation is so obvious. Why isn't it always so clear in the lives of people? How can we make certain His strength shows forth in our own lives?

Psalm 91

1 He that dwelleth in the secret place of the most High shall abide under the shadow of the Almighty.

2 I will say of the Lord, He is my refuge and my fortress: my God; in him will I trust.

3 Surely he shall deliver thee from the snare of the fowler, and from the noisome pestilence.

4 He shall cover thee with his feathers, and under his wings shalt thou trust: his truth shall be thy shield and buckler.

5 Thou shalt not be afraid for the terror by night; nor for the arrow that flieth by day;

6 Nor for the pestilence that walketh in darkness; nor for the destruction that wasteth at noonday.

7 A thousand shall fall at thy side, and ten thousand at thy right hand; but it shall not come nigh thee.

8 Only with thine eyes shalt thou behold and see the reward of the wicked.

9 Because thou hast made the Lord, which is my refuge, even the most High, thy habitation;

10 There shall no evil befall thee, neither shall any plague come nigh thy dwelling.

11 For he shall give his angels charge over thee, to keep thee in all thy ways.

12 They shall bear thee up in their hands, lest thou dash thy foot against a stone.

13 Thou shalt tread upon the lion and adder: the young lion and the dragon shalt thou trample under feet.

14 Because he hath set his love upon me, therefore will I deliver him: I will set him on high, because he hath known my name.

15 He shall call upon me, and I will answer him: I will be with him in trouble; I will deliver him, and honour him.

16 With long life will I satisfy him, and shew him my salvation.

Psalm 95

1 O come, let us sing unto the Lord: let us make a joyful noise to the rock of our salvation.

2 Let us come before his presence with thanksgiving, and make a joyful noise unto him with psalms.

3 For the Lord is a great God, and a great King above all gods.

4 In his hand are the deep places of the earth: the strength of the hills is his also.

5 The sea is his, and he made it: and his hands formed the dry land.

6 O come, let us worship and bow down: let us kneel before the Lord our maker.

7 For he is our God; and we are the people of his pasture, and the sheep of his hand. To day if ye will hear his voice,

8 Harden not your heart, as in the provocation, and as in the day of temptation in the wilderness:

9 When your fathers tempted me, proved me, and saw my work.

10 Forty years long was I grieved with this generation, and said, It is a people that do err in their heart, and they have not known my ways:

11 Unto whom I sware in my wrath that they should not enter into my rest.

For Your Information

"Secret place": place near God, the temple.

"Snare of the fowler": a word picture for the trap of an enemy.

"Noisome": noxious, deadly.

"Cover thee with his feathers": as a hen protects her chicks.

"The day of temptation in the wilderness": refers to Meribah and Massah, names meaning "rebellion" and "testing," given to a place where the Hebrews rebelled against God and His prophet Moses (Exodus 17:7).

"Rest": the Promised Land, also the rest of eternal life with God.

Psalm 91

This orphan psalm describes God's protection for His people. The first half pictures the safety of believers as they make God their refuge.

Verses 5–7 provide examples of terrors God deflects from believers, who will see the destruction of their enemies.

The second half parallels the first as it describes God's favors for the faithful. His people will not be destroyed, no matter what the world throws their way.

• Compare the protections God offers in the first and second parts of this psalm. What verses seem to have a connection or further explain earlier ones? Can you categorize all the overall threats to the Christian?

Psalm 95

Another orphan psalm calls the people to worship God, the foundation of their salvation. Using descriptions of the earth, the psalmist declares God's authority over all things.

The second half of the psalm calls believers to submission before this glorious Lord and warns against rebellion, as the Hebrews of the Exodus fought against Moses and God in the desert. Because they did not trust God, the psalmist reminds us, God did not let them into His Promised Land.

• What does it mean to submit to God? Can you name some ways people yield to His power? What are some benefits of obedience to Him?

Psalm 96

1 O sing unto the Lord a new song: sing unto the Lord, all the earth.

2 Sing unto the Lord, bless his name; shew forth his salvation from day to day.

3 Declare his glory among the heathen, his wonders among all people.

4 For the Lord is great, and greatly to be praised: he is to be feared above all gods.

5 For all the gods of the nations are idols: but the Lord made the heavens.

6 Honour and majesty are before him: strength and beauty are in his sanctuary.

7 Give unto the Lord, O ye kindreds of the people, give unto the Lord glory and strength.

8 Give unto the Lord the glory due unto his name: bring an offering, and come into his courts.

9 O worship the Lord in the beauty of holiness: fear before him, all the earth.

10 Say among the heathen that the Lord reigneth: the world also shall be established that it shall not be moved: he shall judge the people righteously.

11 Let the heavens rejoice, and let the earth be glad; let the sea roar, and the fulness thereof.

12 Let the field be joyful, and all that is therein: then shall all the trees of the wood rejoice

13 Before the Lord: for he cometh, for he cometh to judge the earth: he shall judge the world with righteousness, and the people with his truth.

Psalm 97

1 The Lord reigneth; let the earth rejoice; let the multitude of isles be glad thereof.

2 Clouds and darkness are round about him: righteousness and judgment are the habitation of his throne.

3 A fire goeth before him, and burneth up his enemies round about.

4 His lightnings enlightened the world: the earth saw, and trembled.

5 The hills melted like wax at the presence of the Lord, at the presence of the Lord of the whole earth.

6 The heavens declare his righteousness, and all the people see his glory.

7 Confounded be all they that serve graven images, that boast themselves of idols: worship him, all ye gods.

8 Zion heard, and was glad; and the daughters of Judah rejoiced because of thy judgments, O Lord.

9 For thou, Lord, art high above all the earth: thou art exalted far above all gods.

10 Ye that love the Lord, hate evil: he preserveth the souls of his saints; he delivereth them out of the hand of the wicked.

11 Light is sown for the righteous, and gladness for the upright in heart.

12 Rejoice in the Lord, ye righteous; and give thanks at the remembrance of his holiness.

For Your Information

"New song": a song glorifying God's new mercies.

"Show forth": declare the news of.

"Honor and majesty": These are personified as His attendants.

"In the beauty of holiness": recognizing the beauty of God's holiness.

"Multitude of isles": many or great isles.

"Clouds and darkness": reminders that God's holiness must be vailed.

"Fire": symbolic of God's wrath.

"Graven images": carved idols.

"Daughters of Judah": the people of Judah.

"Light is sown": enough light for His people to follow God is available to them daily.

Psalm 96

Based on 1 Chronicles 16:23–34, Psalm 96, an orphan psalm, calls on the faithful to sing to God, declaring His glory to all people. The Old Testament era was not one of great missionary activity, and this psalm prefigures the New Testament Gospel that would be preached to all peoples. It clearly denies the value of all other gods, who do not have the Lord's authority over creation, and summons all people to worship the Lord alone.

The second half of the psalm outlines the glories for which He should be praised and calls those with faith to declare them to the heathen. The entire creation rejoices at God's reign as it looks forward to His final judgment.

• Should God's glory be preached to all peoples? Why? If we do not take some part in the mission, do we truly appreciate His mercy? Name a few ways we can accomplish that mission.

Psalm 97

Again an orphan psalm calls God's faithful people to worship Him for His rule over the earth. His holiness, veiled from human view, is so awesome, none can stand to see it. Like fire and lightning, it can induce fear. Indeed all his creation again tells of His righteousness.

Anyone worshiping idols will be put to shame, but God's people rejoice at His authority, and He will be praised and obeyed. God lights the paths of His people, and they rejoice in Him.

• Some concepts in this psalm should be familiar to you, because they have appeared in previous psalms. Identify those concepts, using a concordance, if you have one. Why does God repeat these ideas in scripture? What should your response be?

Psalm 98

1 O sing unto the Lord a new song; for he hath done marvellous things: his right hand, and his holy arm, hath gotten him the victory.

2 The Lord hath made known his salvation: his righteousness hath he openly shewed in the sight of the heathen.

3 He hath remembered his mercy and his truth toward the house of Israel: all the ends of the earth have seen the salvation of our God.

4 Make a joyful noise unto the Lord, all the earth: make a loud noise, and rejoice, and sing praise.

5 Sing unto the Lord with the harp; with the harp, and the voice of a psalm.

6 With trumpets and sound of cornet make a joyful noise before the Lord, the King.

7 Let the sea roar, and the fulness thereof; the world, and they that dwell therein.

8 Let the floods clap their hands: let the hills be joyful together

9 Before the Lord; for he cometh to judge the earth: with righteousness shall he judge the world, and the people with equity.

Psalm 100

1 Make a joyful noise unto the Lord, all ye lands.

2 Serve the Lord with gladness: come before his presence with singing.

3 Know ye that the Lord he is God: it is he that hath made us, and not we ourselves; we are his people, and the sheep of his pasture.

4 Enter into his gates with thanksgiving, and into his courts with praise: be thankful unto him, and bless his name.

5 For the Lord is good; his mercy is everlasting; and his truth endureth to all generations.

For Your Information

"Marvellous things": He has done them in the work of redemption.

"All the earth": all the people of the earth.

"Serve the Lord with gladness": worship Him with joy.

"Gates": the temple gates.

"Courts": the temple courts.

Psalm 98

Beginning and ending in words similar to the start and finish of Psalm 96, this praise psalm appropriately follows the previous one, as it continues to praise God's reign over His people.

God has revealed Himself, through His salvation, to all people, and the covenant with Israel has been an example that all have seen. The psalmist calls upon all people to loudly praise Him with voices and instruments. Even the earth rejoices at the coming of the Lord to judge the earth.

• Has God worked a marvelous work of redemption in your life? How can you tell? Take an opportunity to share what God has done with someone this week.

Psalm 100

Ending the series of royal psalms, these verses rejoice in worship of the king who has been described in the former psalms. Again all people are called to join the celebration of God's power and faithfulness towards His people.

• Read over the kingly psalms we have been studying this week. What common themes do they have? What ideas about praise can you glean from them? How can that help your personal worship?

Psalm 101

1 I will sing of mercy and judgment: unto thee, O Lord, will I sing.

2 I will behave myself wisely in a perfect way. O when wilt thou come unto me? I will walk within my house with a perfect heart.

3 I will set no wicked thing before mine eyes: I hate the work of them that turn aside; it shall not cleave to me.

4 A froward heart shall depart from me: I will not know a wicked person.

5 Whoso privily slandereth his neighbour, him will I cut off: him that hath an high look and a proud heart will not I suffer.

6 Mine eyes shall be upon the faithful of the land, that they may dwell with me: he that walketh in a perfect way, he shall serve me.

7 He that worketh deceit shall not dwell within my house: he that telleth lies shall not tarry in my sight.

8 I will early destroy all the wicked of the land; that I may cut off all wicked doers from the city of the Lord.

Psalm 103

1 Bless the Lord, O my soul: and all that is within me, bless his holy name.

2 . . .And forget not all his benefits:

3 Who forgiveth all thine iniquities; who healeth all thy diseases;

4 Who redeemeth thy life from destruction; who crowneth thee with lovingkindness and tender mercies;

5 Who satisfieth thy mouth with good things; so that thy youth is renewed like the eagle's.

6 The Lord executeth righteousness and judgment for all that are oppressed.

7 He made known his ways unto Moses, his acts unto the children of Israel.

8 The Lord is merciful and gracious, slow to anger, and plenteous in mercy.

9 He will not always chide: neither will he keep his anger for ever.

10 He hath not dealt with us after our sins. . . .

11 For as the heaven is high above the earth, so great is his mercy. . . .

12 As far as the east is from the west, so far hath he removed our transgressions from us.

13 Like as a father pitieth his children, so the Lord pitieth them that fear him.

14 For he knoweth our frame; he remembereth that we are dust.

15 As for man. . .as a flower of the field, so he flourisheth.

16 For the wind passeth over it, and it is gone. . . .

17 But the mercy of the Lord is from everlasting to everlasting upon them that fear him, and his righteousness unto children's children. . . .

19 The Lord hath prepared his throne in the heavens; and his kingdom ruleth over all.

20 Bless the Lord, ye his angels, that excel in strength, that do his commandments, hearkening unto the voice of his word.

21 Bless ye the Lord, all ye his hosts; ye ministers of his, that do his pleasure.

22 Bless the Lord, all his works in all places of his dominion: bless the Lord, O my soul.

For Your Information

"Cleave": cling.

"Froward": perverse.

"Privily": secretly.

"High": haughty.

"Bless": praise.

"Like the eagle's": a bird known for strength and quickness.

"As far as the east is from the west": Since these directions never touch, our sins are wholly forgiven.

Psalm 101

David's psalm shows his desire to live perfectly before God, but only Christ lived a perfect life. Through His Spirit we begin to live more faultlessly on earth, but only in heaven can we gain Christ's purity. When he asks God to come to Him, David recognizes the distance between desire and reality.

David also understands that the people he associates with should also be those who love and follow God, for they influence his thinking and acts. The king promises the wicked will not have a place in his household or country—instead, he will cut them off.

- Do you aspire to the kind of godly life David describes here? What influence will friends have on you? The church? What have you learned from David in these verses?

Psalm 103

David again praises God for His blessings and His mercy. He reminds his readers of good things God has given them personally and corporately as He has dealt with them mercifully, despite their sins.

Through Christ's sacrifice, the God who judges us is blots out our sins and shares a close, loving relationship with us. Though our days fly by, and we finish our bloom quickly, His compassion allows those who love Him live for eternity.

Reminding his readers of God's reign, David calls all beings in heaven and earth to praise Him.

- Are you daily aware of God's mercy on your life? How has He redeemed and satisfied you? What other mercies have you experienced? Have you thanked God for them?

Psalm 102

1 Hear my prayer, O Lord, and let my cry come unto thee.

2 Hide not thy face from me in the day when I am in trouble; incline thine ear unto me: in the day when I call answer me speedily.

3 For my days are consumed like smoke, and my bones are burned as an hearth.

4 My heart is smitten, and withered like grass; so that I forget to eat my bread.

5 By reason of the voice of my groaning my bones cleave to my skin.

6 I am like a pelican of the wilderness: I am like an owl of the desert.

7 I watch, and am as a sparrow alone upon the house top.

8 Mine enemies reproach me all the day; and they that are mad against me are sworn against me.

9 For I have eaten ashes like bread, and mingled my drink with weeping.

10 Because of thine indignation and thy wrath: for thou hast lifted me up, and cast me down.

11 My days are like a shadow that declineth; and I am withered like grass.

12 But thou, O Lord, shalt endure forever; and thy remembrance unto all generations.

13 Thou shalt arise, and have mercy upon Zion: for the time to favour her, yea, the set time, is come.

14 For thy servants take pleasure in her stones, and favour the dust thereof.

15 So the heathen shall fear the name of the Lord, and all the kings of the earth thy glory.

16 When the Lord shall build up Zion, he shall appear in his glory.

17 He will regard the prayer of the destitute, and not despise their prayer.

18 This shall be written for the generation to come: and the people which shall be created shall praise the Lord.

19 For he hath looked down from the height of his sanctuary; from heaven did the Lord behold the earth;

20 To hear the groaning of the prisoner; to loose those that are appointed to death;

21 To declare the name of the Lord in Zion, and his praise in Jerusalem;

22 When the people are gathered together, and the kingdoms, to serve the Lord.

23 He Weakened my strength in the way; he shortened my days.

24 I said, O my God, take me not away in the midst of my days: thy years are throughout all generations.

25 Of old hast thou laid the foundation of the earth: and the heavens are the work of thy hands.

26 They shall perish, but thou shalt endure: yea, all of them shall wax old like a garment; as a vesture shalt thou change them, and they shall be changed:

27 But thou art the same, and thy years shall have no end.

28 The children of thy servants shall continue, and their seed shall be established before thee.

For Your Information

"Consumed like smoke": a word picture of their ephemeral nature.

"My bones cleave to my skin": I am skin and bones.

"Pelican. . .owl. . .sparrow": symbols of loneliness.

"Sworn against me": made his name a curse word.

"Ashes": symbolizes grief.

"The set time": the time promised by God.

"Wax": become.

"Vesture": robe.

"Established before thee": established as God's children.

Psalm 102

This prayer of the afflicted begins with an appeal to God to listen to the psalmist's troubles and respond quickly. Then he details his physical and emotional anguish (verses 3–11).

Though the psalmist is weak, he recognizes that God is not. And in His appointed time, God will have mercy on Zion, which is so beloved by His people that even the dust of her stones is important to them. God will use His power against the heathen when He rebuilds the city. He will hear the cries of His people and respond. Succeeding generations will know of His response, for a record will be kept of it. The psalmist declares God's faithfulness in responding to His hurting people.

Though the psalmist has suffered, he has not lost faith that God will respond. Perishable creation is His work, but He does not change. His promises to Israel will be kept.

• Are you tempted to doubt God when you are in distress? Prepare yourself by remembering God's faithfulness to you. What can you praise Him for doing in your life? How has He protected you?

Psalm 104

1 Bless the Lord, O my soul. O Lord my God, thou art very great. . . .

2 Who coverest thyself with light as with a garment: who stretchest out the heavens like a curtain:

3 Who layeth the beams of his chambers in the waters: who maketh the clouds his chariot: who walketh upon the wings of the wind:

4 Who maketh his angels spirits; his ministers a flaming fire:

5 Who laid the foundations of the earth. . . .

6 Thou coveredst it with the deep as with a garment: the waters stood above the mountains.

7 At thy rebuke they fled; at the voice of thy thunder they hasted away.

8 They go up by the mountains; they go down by the valleys. . . .

9 Thou hast set a bound that they may not pass over. . . .

10 He sendeth the springs into the valleys, which run among the hills.

11 They give drink to every beast of the field: the wild asses quench their thirst.

12 By them shall the fowls of the heaven have their habitation, which sing among the branches.

13 He watereth the hills from his chambers: the earth is satisfied with the fruit of thy works.

14 He causeth the grass to grow for the cattle, and herb for the service of man: that he may bring forth food out of the earth;

15 And wine that maketh glad the heart of man, and oil to make his face to shine, and bread which strengtheneth man's heart.

16 The trees of the Lord are full of sap. . . .

17 Where the birds make their nests. . . .

18 The high hills are a refuge for the wild goats. . . .

19 He appointed the moon for seasons: the sun knoweth his going down.

20 Thou makest darkness, . . .wherein all the beasts of the forest do creep forth.

21 The young lions roar after their prey, and seek their meat from God.

22 The sun ariseth, they gather themselves together, and lay them down in their dens.

23 Man goeth forth unto his work and to his labour until the evening.

24 O Lord, how manifold are thy works! . . .the earth is full of thy riches.

25 So is this great and wide sea, wherein are things creeping innumerable. . . .

26 There. . .is that leviathan, whom thou hast made to play therein.

27 These wait all upon thee; that thou mayest give them their meat in due season. . . .

29 Thou hidest thy face, they are troubled: thou takest away their breath, they die. . . .

30 Thou sendest forth thy spirit, they are created: and thou renewest the face of the earth.

31 The glory of the Lord shall endure for ever: the Lord shall rejoice in his works.

32 He looketh on the earth, and it trembleth: he toucheth the hills, and they smoke.

34 My meditation of him shall be sweet: I will be glad in the Lord.

35 Let the sinners be consumed out of the earth. . . . Praise ye the Lord.

For Your Information

"Who coverest thyself with light as with a garment": who is enrobed in light, indicating God's glory.

"Chambers": as the upper chambers of a heavenly house.

"In the waters": above the rainwaters.

"Ministers": agents (the wind and fire).

"Rebuke": majestic command.

"Hasted": hastened.

"Manifold": many, with great variety.

"Leviathan": a mythic sea monster.

Psalm 104

The psalmist, possibly David, follows in Moses' footsteps as he praises God for His creation. The days outlined in Genesis 1 are spoken of poetically here: verses 1–6, creation of light and the firmament (days 1 and 2 of creation); verses 7–18, plants (day 3); verses 19–23, heavenly bodies (day 4); verses 24–30, sea life and earthly creatures (days 5 and 6). Though they are wonderful, the psalmist warns that all parts of creation are temporary. The psalm ends with praise for the eternal Creator, who has made them all and rules over them, and the hope that the wicked will be eradicated from the earth.

• To fully appreciate this psalm, read the first chapter of the book of Genesis. How is this psalm like it? How is it different? How do they both help you understand God's glory and praise Him?

WEEK TEN

Introduction

This week we cover quite a bit of ground, discussing Psalms 108 to 119. Many are orphan praise psalms. Though we may feel curious about the names of those who wrote them, there can be no doubt as to why they are included here. Whether they are psalms of David, as some commentators guess, or of another psalmist, they provide fine worship, instruction, and meditation. Not knowing the author's name cannot diminish the value of the verses.

In Psalms 108 and 118 we see a frequent poetic convention we've noticed before in this book. In Psalm 108, parts of previous psalms are repeated. In 118, a single idea is repeated a number of times for emphasis. We may be able to understand this when God has done something wonderful for us or taught us a terrific new truth about Himself. Over and over we want to share what He has done in our lives, and we want it to impact others powerfully. Repetition should not be a cue for us to tune out, but to tune in clearly to the reality before us. Then perhaps we can join the psalmist's excitement for God.

At 176 verses, Psalm 119 is the longest psalm and longest chapter in the Bible. We cannot cover it all here, so selections have been chosen to give readers the flavor of the psalm and some help in understanding it.

This psalm, which focuses on God's Word, uses eight Hebrew words to describe the scripture: precepts, statutes, commandments, and so on. Only two verses in the whole psalm do not provide some description of God's Word. That repetition, too, should provide us with some clue about how important His scriptures are to God and should also be to anyone who wants to follow Him closely.

In the original Hebrew language, the verses of Psalm 119 form an acrostic, with a section for each of the twenty-two letters of the Hebrew alphabet. In many Bibles, the letter is indicated at the head of each section of eight verses. We will cover *aleph, beth, gimel,* then skip to *he,* and finish with *tau,* at the end of the psalm. Of course none of the verses left out have been done so because they are unimportant, and I encourage readers to spend time in the missing verses to enjoy the entire psalm.

Psalm 108

1 O God, my heart is fixed; I will sing and give praise, even with my glory.

2 Awake, psaltery and harp: I myself will awake early.

3 I will praise thee, O Lord, among the people: and I will sing praises unto thee among the nations.

4 For thy mercy is great above the heavens: and thy truth reacheth unto the clouds.

5 Be thou exalted, O God, above the heavens: and thy glory above all the earth;

6 That thy beloved may be delivered: save with thy right hand, and answer me.

7 God hath spoken in his holiness; I will rejoice, I will divide Shechem, and mete out the valley of Succoth.

8 Gilead is mine; Manasseh is mine; Ephraim also is the strength of mine head; Judah is my lawgiver;

9 Moab is my washpot; over Edom will I cast out my shoe; over Philistia will I triumph.

10 Who will bring me into the strong city? who will lead me into Edom?

11 Wilt not thou, O God, who hast cast us off? and wilt not thou, O God, go forth with our hosts?

12 Give us help from trouble: for vain is the help of man.

13 Through God we shall do valiantly: for he it is that shall tread down our enemies.

Psalm 110

1 The Lord said unto my Lord, Sit thou at my right hand, until I make thine enemies thy footstool.

2 The Lord shall send the rod of thy strength out of Zion: rule thou in the midst of thine enemies.

3 Thy people shall be willing in the day of thy power, in the beauties of holiness from the womb of the morning: thou hast the dew of thy youth.

4 The Lord hath sworn, and will not repent, Thou art a priest for ever after the order of Melchizedek.

5 The Lord at thy right hand shall strike through kings in the day of his wrath.

6 He shall judge among the heathen, he shall fill the places with the dead bodies; he shall wound the heads over many countries.

7 He shall drink of the brook in the way: therefore shall he lift up the head.

For Your Information

"Fixed": set on God.

"Thy beloved": God's nation.

"I will divide": God will give His people the foreign places listed in the psalm.

"Shechem. . .Succoth. . .Gilead": places east of the Jordan that Israel, though God's power, conquered.

"Manasseh": part the land of Mannaseh was east of the Jordan.

"Ephraim. . .Judah": two of Israel's leading tribes.

"Moab. . .Edom. . .Philistia": some of Israel's enemies.

"My Lord": my sovereign.

"Right hand": a place of honor, beside the king.

"Make thine enemies thy footstool": put them under your feet as a conquered enemy.

"Rod": scepter.

"Thy people shall be willing": They will be willing to go into battle.

"Repent": change His mind.

"Melchizedek": a king-priest in Abraham's time (Genesis 14:18–20).

"Strike through": destroy.

"Drink of the brook": Scholars differ on the meaning of this somewhat obscure phrase. Some see it as a symbol of refreshment, others as a picture of Jesus' sacrifice for our redemption.

"Lift up the head": a sign of victory.

Psalm 108

Another psalm of David, this combines Psalm 57:7–11 (verses 1–5), with Psalm 60:5–12 (verses 6–13). The psalmist opens with praise for God and declares His mercies. Then he asks for God's deliverance from enemies and recounts God's promise to give the land to Israel.

Verses 10–13 show his response to those promises: He will trust in God to give Israel the victory, help in time of trouble. Only through Him can they be victorious.

• Why is it important to praise God in times of trouble? How does it affect our hearts and spirits?

Psalm 110

This unique psalm of David clearly prophesies the coming of the Messiah, who, unlike David, combines the roles of king and priest in one person. David, though he was both prophet and king, did not hold the position of priest. Here he speaks of one greater than he, with immense earthly and spiritual authority. The final verses describe the Messiah as a warrior who shall judge the world with His battles and achieve the final righteous victory.

• What does Christ being king and priest together mean? How does that impact a believer's thought life? Actions?

Psalm 111

1 Praise ye the Lord. I will praise the Lord with my whole heart, in the assembly of the upright, and in the congregation.

2 The works of the Lord are great, sought out of all them that have pleasure therein.

3 His work is honourable and glorious: and his righteousness endureth for ever.

4 He hath made his wonderful works to be remembered: the Lord is gracious and full of compassion.

5 He hath given meat unto them that fear him: he will ever be mindful of his covenant.

6 He hath shewed his people the power of his works, that he may give them the heritage of the heathen.

7 The works of his hands are verity and judgment; all his commandments are sure.

8 They stand fast for ever and ever, and are done in truth and uprightness.

9 He sent redemption unto his people: he hath commanded his covenant for ever: holy and reverend is his name.

10 The fear of the Lord is the beginning of wisdom: a good understanding have all they that do his commandments: his praise endureth for ever.

Psalm 112

1 Praise ye the Lord. Blessed is the man that feareth the Lord, that delighteth greatly in his commandments.

2 His seed shall be mighty upon earth: the generation of the upright shall be blessed.

3 Wealth and riches shall be in his house: and his righteousness endureth for ever.

4 Unto the upright there ariseth light in the darkness: he is gracious, and full of compassion, and righteous.

5 A good man sheweth favour, and lendeth: he will guide his affairs with discretion.

6 Surely he shall not be moved for ever: the righteous shall be in everlasting remembrance.

7 He shall not be afraid of evil tidings: his heart is fixed, trusting in the Lord.

8 His heart is established, he shall not be afraid, until he see his desire upon his enemies.

9 He hath dispersed, he hath given to the poor; his righteousness endureth for ever; his horn shall be exalted with honour.

10 The wicked shall see it, and be grieved; he shall gnash with his teeth, and melt away: the desire of the wicked shall perish.

For Your Information

"Praise ye the Lord": Hallelujah, in Hebrew.

"Assembly of the upright": those who truly believe in God.

"He hath given meat": He provides food (see also Matthew 6:11).

"The heritage of the heathen": God will give the inheritance of those who do not accept Him to His people.

"Verity": truth.

"Fear": awe.

"Beginning": This also has the sense of "chief."

"Seed": descendants.

"Light": help, relief.

"Evil tidings": bad news.

"Dispersed": give generously.

"Established": set in God's principles.

"Gnash his teeth": a sign of malevolence.

Psalm 111

This begins a series of praise orphan psalms that last through Psalm 118. The entire psalm praises the works of God, as he blesses his people in many ways. Those who hold God in awe are wise. For knowing His power will influence their whole lives and give good judgment. As a result God will be praised for His greatness.

- What kinds of works does God do? List the ones identified in this psalm. If you need to know if God is working in a situation, can this information help you?

- What difference does God's wisdom make in a person's life? In thinking? In actions? In attitude?

Psalm 112

Another orphan praise psalm that begins with the word "hallelujah," this describes the blessings God pours out on the faithful. In response the believer lives in a manner that honors God, giving in return and living without fear.

- What blessings does God gives the righteous? Describe what God gives and the response of the believer to those gifts.

- What reaction does the faithful person have to trouble? Have you seen the wicked in trouble? How do they often respond? What makes the difference? If a faithful person does not respond well to trouble, what could it mean?

Psalm 113

1 Praise ye the Lord. Praise, O ye servants of the Lord, praise the name of the Lord.

2 Blessed be the name of the Lord from this time forth and for evermore.

3 From the rising of the sun unto the going down of the same the Lord's name is to be praised.

4 The Lord is high above all nations, and his glory above the heavens.

5 Who is like unto the Lord our God, who dwelleth on high,

6 Who humbleth himself to behold the things that are in heaven, and in the earth!

7 He raiseth up the poor out of the dust, and lifteth the needy out of the dunghill;

8 That he may set him with princes, even with the princes of his people.

9 He maketh the barren woman to keep house, and to be a joyful mother of children. Praise ye the Lord.

Psalm 115

1 Not unto us, O Lord, not unto us, but unto thy name give glory, for thy mercy, and for thy truth's sake.

2 Wherefore should the heathen say, Where is now their God?

3 But our God is in the heavens: he hath done whatsoever he hath pleased.

4 Their idols are silver and gold, the work of men's hands.

5 They have mouths, but they speak not: eyes have they, but they see not:

6 They have ears, but they hear not: noses have they, but they smell not:

7 They have hands, but they handle not: feet have they, but they walk not: neither speak they through their throat.

8 They that make them are like unto them; so is every one that trusteth in them.

9 O Israel, trust thou in the Lord: he is their help and their shield.

10 O house of Aaron, trust in the Lord: he is their help and their shield.

11 Ye that fear the Lord, trust in the Lord: he is their help and their shield.

12 The Lord hath been mindful of us: he will bless us; he will bless the house of Israel; he will bless the house of Aaron.

13 He will bless them that fear the Lord, both small and great.

14 The Lord shall increase you more and more, you and your children.

15 Ye are blessed of the Lord which made heaven and earth.

16 The heaven, even the heavens, are the Lord's: but the earth hath he given to the children of men.

17 The dead praise not the Lord, neither any that go down into silence.

18 But we will bless the Lord from this time forth and for evermore. Praise the Lord.

For Your Information

"Servants of the Lord": His people.

"High above all nations": God is above all pagan gods, made of stone and wood.

"The heavens": the physical heavenly bodies, not God's eternal home.

"The barren woman to keep house": literally, "the barren woman of the house," not a command to do housekeeping. In the ancient Old Testament culture, barrenness was a terrible misfortune.

"Wherefore": why.

"Heavens": the place of God's enthronement.

"Shield": protector.

"Increase": in numbers and prosperity.

"The dead": Some commentators believe this is describes physical death. Others believe it is those who die without knowing God.

"Down into silence": into the afterworld without God, where he is not praised.

Psalm 113

An unknown psalmist calls God's people to praise Him, from morning to night, across the earth, for He is powerful and glorious. Though He is far above the earthly realm, He cares for the person in need. He cares for the poor and improves their position and makes the barren woman fruitful.

• God's humility in attending to the needs of humanity is very great. How can humility make even the most powerful being more honored? How can we follow in God's footsteps?

Psalm 115

The God described in Psalm 113 is nothing like the pagan gods described in the first half of this psalm. Unbelievers have no reason to denigrate the Lord, since their gods are created beings, made of silver and gold, that cannot respond to their worshipers.

But God helps and blesses His people, as He rules over them, and they praise Him for it.

• People often talk about having "a personal relationship with Jesus." How is it obvious that this psalmist has that kind of relationship with God? What does he know about God? How has God affected his life?

Psalm 114

1 When Israel went out of Egypt, the house of Jacob from a people of strange language;

  2 Judah was his sanctuary, and Israel his dominion.

  3 The sea saw it, and fled: Jordan was driven back.

  4 The mountains skipped like rams, and the little hills like lambs.

  5 What ailed thee, O thou sea, that thou fleddest? thou Jordan, that thou wast driven back?

  6 Ye mountains, that ye skipped like rams; and ye little hills, like lambs?

  7 Tremble, thou earth, at the presence of the Lord, at the presence of the God of Jacob;

  8 Which turned the rock into a standing water, the flint into a fountain of waters.

Psalm 117

1 O praise the Lord, all ye nations: praise him, all ye people.

  2 For his merciful kindness is great toward us: and the truth of the Lord endureth for ever. Praise ye the Lord.

For Your Information

"Out of Egypt": in the Exodus.

"Strange language": foreign language.

"Judah. . .Israel": a parallel reference to the two parts of God's nation as a single people. Jerusalem was in Judah, where the temple would be built, thus it is God's sanctuary.

"Sea. . .Jordan": the Red Sea and Jordan River.

"Skipped like rams": a poetical description of the motion of a mountain forest, showing the land's awe at God's works.

"Wast": were.

"Tremble": a sign of awe.

"Rock into a standing water. . .fountain of waters": references to Exodus 17:6 and Numbers 20:11, at Massah and Meribah, where God brought water from dry rocks.

Psalm 114

Another orphan psalm celebrates the Exodus, when God brought His people from Egypt into the Promised Land. Leaving Egypt, the Hebrews were backed up to the Red Sea, cornered by the Egyptians. God caused the sea to part so they could escape (Exodus 14). Again God parts the Jordan River, as they cross into the new land (Joshua 3). The land itself quakes at God's being there.

• Israel has a long memory of the events of the Exodus and continues to glorify God for what He did for them. The story was passed down through the generations. Is there something God has done for you that you want to pass on to your children? What truths would it show them about God?

Psalm 117

Here is the shortest chapter in the Bible, with only two verses. It glorifies God and in a few words sets before us two reasons for praise: God's mercy and His truth. It is simple enough to understand, and we need to keep those truths ever before us.

• Do we keep the truths of God's mercy and truth before us? What does that entail? How will they affect our lives?

Psalm 116

1 I love the Lord, because he hath heard my voice and my supplications.

2 Because he hath inclined his ear unto me, therefore will I call upon him as long as I live.

3 The sorrows of death compassed me, and the pains of hell gat hold upon me: I found trouble and sorrow.

4 Then called I upon the name of the Lord; O Lord, I beseech thee, deliver my soul.

5 Gracious is the Lord, and righteous; yea, our God is merciful.

6 The Lord preserveth the simple: I was brought low, and he helped me.

7 Return unto thy rest, O my soul; for the Lord hath dealt bountifully with thee.

8 For thou hast delivered my soul from death, mine eyes from tears, and my feet from falling.

9 I will walk before the Lord in the land of the living.

10 I believed, therefore have I spoken: I was greatly afflicted:

11 I said in my haste, All men are liars.

12 What shall I render unto the Lord for all his benefits toward me?

13 I will take the cup of salvation, and call upon the name of the Lord.

14 I will pay my vows unto the Lord now in the presence of all his people.

15 Precious in the sight of the Lord is the death of his saints.

16 O Lord, truly I am thy servant; I am thy servant, and the son of thine handmaid: thou hast loosed my bonds.

17 I will offer to thee the sacrifice of thanksgiving, and will call upon the name of the Lord.

18 I will pay my vows unto the Lord now in the presence of all his people.

19 In the courts of the Lord's house, in the midst of thee, O Jerusalem. Praise ye the Lord.

For Your Information

"Supplications": prayers.

"Compassed": surrounded.

"Gat": got.

"Simple": those who simply trust God.

"Rest": peace with God.

"Feet from falling": a poetic way of saying falling into sin.

"Walk before the Lord": live in His favor.

"I said in my haste": He quickly decides all men are liars, but he was wrong.

"Cup of salvation": a drink offering, part of the temple worship. He worships God with his renewed life.

"Precious": watched over. In His mercy, no one dies before God's time.

"Handmaid": a female servant. He claims intimate relationship with God, as he has grown up in His household.

Psalm 116

Because God saved this unknown psalmist and answered his prayers, he comes to love Him deeply. The psalms are not a mystery, in which we must wait for the end to find out what happened. They often declare their motives up front, so readers can praise God along with the psalmist.

The psalmist then describes the events that caused the praise. He was near death, feeling the terrors of hell and experiencing trouble, when he called on God to save his soul. God responded not only by saving the psalmist's soul, but by rescuing his body, too. He returns to life determined to live faithfully for God. He will do all that is required for the faithful believer, including worshiping at the temple.

• When God does something wonderful for you, does it make you love Him more or do you take Him for granted? Is there anything you need to thank Him for? Do you need to renew your faithfulness to Him? We all find it easy to slip in small ways that may powerfully impact our spiritual lives. Take this time to renew your love for Jesus, if you have slipped.

Psalm 118

1 O give thanks unto the Lord; for he is good: because his mercy endureth for ever.

2 Let Israel now say, that his mercy endureth for ever.

3 Let the house of Aaron now say, that his mercy endureth for ever.

4 Let them now that fear the Lord say, that his mercy endureth for ever.

5 I called upon the Lord in distress: the Lord answered me, and set me in a large place.

6 The Lord is on my side; I will not fear: what can man do unto me?

7 The Lord taketh my part with them that help me: therefore shall I see my desire upon them that hate me.

8 It is better to trust in the Lord than to put confidence in man.

9 It is better to trust in the Lord than to put confidence in princes.

10 All nations compassed me about: but in the name of the Lord will I destroy them.

11 They compassed me about; yea, they compassed me about: but in the name of the Lord I will destroy them.

12 They compassed me about like bees: they are quenched as the fire of thorns: for in the name of the Lord I will destroy them.

13 Thou hast thrust sore at me that I might fall: but the Lord helped me.

14 The Lord is my strength and song, and is become my salvation.

15 The voice of rejoicing and salvation is in the tabernacles of the righteous: the right hand of the Lord doeth valiantly.

16 The right hand of the Lord is exalted: the right hand of the Lord doeth valiantly.

17 I shall not die, but live, and declare the works of the Lord.

18 The Lord hath chastened me sore: but he hath not given me over unto death.

19 Open to me the gates of righteousness: I will go into them, and I will praise the Lord:

20 This gate of the Lord, into which the righteous shall enter.

21 I will praise thee: for thou hast heard me, and art become my salvation.

22 The stone which the builders refused is become the head stone of the corner.

23 This is the Lord's doing; it is marvellous in our eyes.

24 This is the day which the Lord hath made; we will rejoice and be glad in it.

25 Save now, I beseech thee, O Lord: O Lord, I beseech thee, send now prosperity.

26 Blessed be he that cometh in the name of the Lord: we have blessed you out of the house of the Lord.

27 God is the Lord, which hath shewed us light: bind the sacrifice with cords, even unto the horns of the altar.

28 Thou art my God, and I will praise thee: thou art my God, I will exalt thee.

29 O give thanks unto the Lord; for he is good: for his mercy endureth for ever.

For Your Information

"Large place": a wide place, one where he moves about with freedom.

"Compassed me about": surrounded me.

"Bees": painful irritants.

"Fire of thorns": suddenly, since a fire built of thorns burned quickly.

"Strength and song": God gives him power to overcome his enemies and a victory song of praise.

"Right hand of the Lord is exalted": God's power is lifted up, a sign of great authority.

"Sore": sorely.

"Gate of the Lord": to the temple court.

"Stone": either the king or Israel, either of which was denigrated by the enemy.

"Head stone of the corner": capstone.

Psalm 118

Though we do not know what events caused the praise, in the first four verses of this liturgical orphan psalm, the king calls his people to give thanks to God for His mercy in saving Israel.

Verses 5–18 describe the confidence the psalmist had in God, the battle he engaged in, and the victory the Lord brought. In the next section, verses 19–21, the victor asks to enter the temple, to worship. Verses 22–27, spoken by the priests and people, praise God for bringing salvation through the king. The enemy thought Israel had little strength to defend herself, but they had not counted on God. The Savior gave Israel and her ruler the power to resist, and they praise Him loudly and sing the praises of the anointed ruler.

In the final two verses, the king exalts God and praises Him, ending by repeating the words of the first four verses, proclaiming that God's mercy endures eternally.

- What does it mean for God's mercy to endure forever? To whom is His mercy extended? What does it mean to experience His mercy?

Psalm 119

1 Blessed are the undefiled in the way, who walk in the law of the Lord.

2 Blessed are they that keep his testimonies, and that seek him with the whole heart.

3 They also do no iniquity: they walk in his ways.

4 Thou hast commanded us to keep thy precepts diligently.

5 O that my ways were directed to keep thy statutes!

6 Then shall I not be ashamed, when I have respect unto all thy commandments.

7 I will praise thee with uprightness of heart, when I shall have learned thy righteous judgments.

8 I will keep thy statutes: O forsake me not utterly.

9 Wherewithal shall a young man cleanse his way? by taking heed thereto according to thy word.

10 With my whole heart have I sought thee: O let me not wander from thy commandments.

11 Thy word have I hid in mine heart, that I might not sin against thee.

12 Blessed art thou, O Lord: teach me thy statutes.

13 With my lips have I declared all the judgments of thy mouth.

14 I have rejoiced in the way of thy testimonies, as much as in all riches.

15 I will meditate in thy precepts, and have respect unto thy ways. I will delight myself in thy statutes: I will not forget thy word.

17 Deal bountifully with thy servant, that I may live, and keep thy word.

18 Open thou mine eyes, that I may behold wondrous things out of thy law.

19 I am a stranger in the earth: hide not thy commandments from me.

20 My soul breaketh for the longing that it hath unto thy judgments at all times.

21 Thou hast rebuked the proud that are cursed, which do err from thy commandments.

22 Remove from me reproach and contempt; for I have kept thy testimonies.

23 Princes also did sit and speak against me: but thy servant did meditate in thy statutes.

24 Thy testimonies also are my delight and my counsellers. . . .

33 Teach me, O Lord, the way of thy statutes; and I shall keep it unto the end.

34 Give me understanding, and I shall keep thy law; yea, I shall observe it with my whole heart.

35 Make me to go in the path of thy commandments; for therein do I delight.

36 Incline my heart unto thy testimonies, and not to covetousness.

37 Turn away mine eyes from beholding vanity; and quicken thou me in thy way.

38 Stablish thy word unto thy servant, who is devoted to thy fear.

39 Turn away my reproach which I fear: for thy judgments are good.

40 Behold, I have longed after thy precepts: quicken me in thy righteousness. . . .

169 Let my cry come near before thee, O Lord: give me understanding according to thy word.

170 Let my supplication come before thee: deliver me according to thy word.

171 My lips shall utter praise, when thou hast taught me thy statutes.

172 My tongue shall speak of thy word: for all thy commandments are righteousness.

173 Let thine hand help me; for I have chosen thy precepts.

174 I have longed for thy salvation, O Lord; and thy law is my delight.

175 Let my soul live, and it shall praise thee; and let thy judgments help me.

176 I have gone astray like a lost sheep; seek thy servant; for I do not forget thy commandments.

For Your Information

"Undefiled in the way": perfect in following God's path.

"Do no iniquity": Those forgiven by God seek to avoid sin in their lives. Because of Christ's sacrifice and forgiveness, no sin is imputed to them.

"Were directed": The human nature does not desire to do God's will. The psalmist struggles between his human desire and the dictates of God's Word.

"In all riches": He compares the spiritual riches of knowing God to physical worldly wealth.

"Stranger in the earth": He is a stranger to the world because his citizenship is in God's heavenly kingdom.

"Reproach and contempt": from unbelievers who slander him.

" 'Stablish": establish.

"Quicken me": give me life.

Psalm 119

The longest chapter of the Bible has no identified writer, but he certainly left us a magnificent collection of verses on an important topic. For how would we know God and how to live for Him, if He had not given us the scriptures?

The psalm begins by declaring the blessings of walking with God according to His commandments. Through God's Word, the psalmist knows how he should live, yet he struggles with his own failure to live purely. He needs God's help to do so.

He instructs the young to follow God, in order to live in God's righteousness. By focusing on God's directions, meditating on them, and taking delight in them, the young man will obey God's covenant commandments.

As he seeks to obey God's laws, the psalmist begins to understand that he is not a worldly being, but a heavenly one, somewhat lost in this world because he does not follow the sinful paths of many of his fellow-men. Though the law is his comfort, it is an offense to the wicked, who in the face of God's rebuke, take out their hatred for God on his follower. However, the psalmist remains faithful to the words of his Lord.

In verses 33–40, the psalmist does not turn his back on God's path, but desires to know more of God's will for him, through His Word. He wants to know more, to obey more, and to avoid sin.

As the psalm ends, in verses 169–176, the psalm writer cries out to God for understanding and asks God to listen to his prayer. He seeks deliverance and offers God praise and his testimony. Ultimately he is aware of his own inability to obey God and asks for His help in fulfilling the law.

- Read through all of Psalm 119, identifying the eight words the psalmist uses to describe God's Word. What do these different words mean? What do they tell you about the scripture and how it can be valuable in your life? What can you learn about God from these words?

WEEK ELEVEN

Introduction

All the psalms in this week's studies—Psalms 120 to 134—are part of a series of songs of ascents or degrees. They cover a range of topics, from commemoration of events in Israel's history to personal issues of sin or home life.

Some commentators believe the songs of ascents were written for people on a pilgrimage to Jerusalem to worship at the temple; perhaps, as some rabbis held, the fifteen psalms stood for the number of steps into the temple (the word Hebrew word for *ascents* means "step"). Others see this as a poetic name or musical term.

Common themes in these pages are trust in God and His protection of His people. These are unchanging, the first as a requirement of faith and the second as a key part of God's nature. We make a decision to trust in God as our Savior and begin the covenant connection with Him. As we daily live that part of our promise, we are challenged to continue in the path we've begun. Sometimes we fail. But God does not. Though our obedience is imperfect, He cannot desert us. Like the Israelites who spent many years in Babylon, He rescues us from a foreign land of sin and doubt. And again we seek to obey Him more perfectly. As it was for Israel, God does not watch us fall and leave us. He ever faithfully works with us, coming to our rescue as long as we will turn to Him.

The psalms also continue to consider the history of Israel. These verses remind readers of the return from captivity (probably from Babylon), and the joys and challenges it brought. God was with His people during both the happy and sad days. It is the same for us. No matter what we experience, God remains faithful, guiding us, when we seek Him.

Psalm 132 remembers the promise of God to David, that an heir of his body would forever be king in Israel. The fulfillment of that promise was not what many would have expected, but it proved the faithfulness of God, despite the failures of the kings in David's line. Though they fell into pagan worship, His promise of a Redeemer did not alter. Jesus came unexpectedly, not because God had changed, but because His people were not watching and waiting for Him.

These psalms touch our hearts, minds, and spirits, if we are open to God's Spirit. May they benefit us, as they perhaps did the pilgrims on their way to worship in the temple.

Psalm 120

1 In my distress I cried unto the Lord, and he heard me.

2 Deliver my soul, O Lord, from lying lips, and from a deceitful tongue.

3 What shall be given unto thee? or what shall be done unto thee, thou false tongue?

4 Sharp arrows of the mighty, with coals of juniper.

5 Woe is me, that I sojourn in Mesech, that I dwell in the tents of Kedar!

6 My soul hath long dwelt with him that hateth peace.

7 I am for peace: but when I speak, they are for war.

Psalm 121

1 I will lift up mine eyes unto the hills, from whence cometh my help.

2 My help cometh from the Lord, which made heaven and earth.

3 He will not suffer thy foot to be moved: he that keepeth thee will not slumber.

4 Behold, he that keepeth Israel shall neither slumber nor sleep.

5 The Lord is thy keeper: the Lord is thy shade upon thy right hand.

6 The sun shall not smite thee by day, nor the moon by night.

7 The Lord shall preserve thee from all evil: he shall preserve thy soul.

8 The Lord shall preserve thy going out and thy coming in from this time forth, and even for evermore.

For Your Information

"Lying lips. . .deceitful tongue. . .false tongue": Malicious words spoken by enemies have harmed the psalmist.

"Sharp arrows": God's response will appropriately be as sharp as the wicked tongue.

"Coals of juniper": They create a hot, long-lasting fire.

"Mesech": a central Asia Minor territory.

"Kedar": an area in Northern Arabia, east of Palestine.

"I am for peace. . . .war": This could either mean that the psalmist is a king who faces battle, or that he is an ordinary man who faces spiritual battles.

"Lift up mine eyes": in desire, hope, and expectation.

"The hills": referring to those around Jerusalem.

"From whence cometh my help": This is actually a question—where does my help come from? It is answered in the next verse.

"Maker of heaven and earth": God the creator.

"Shade": shelter.

Psalm 120

Accused falsely, the psalmist in this psalm of ascents calls out to God for deliverance, asking that the slanderer be punished with God's judgment of arrows and coals. But the harsh words have made the psalmist feel as if he lives in the midst of pagans, far distant from his homeland. Though he would like peace, his enemies lead him into warfare.

• Does this psalm help you understand why God places such importance on a person's words? How can harsh words hurt others? How can kind ones help them? Is there a time when even Christians may need to speak harshly?

Psalm 121

Here an unknown psalmist depicts the many ways God preserves His people. As he looks up to Jerusalem's hills, he recognizes the Lord's constant protection over his life, day and night. Nothing is beyond His protective powers.

• Where does your help come from? Do you turn first to God, in any circumstance? Can you name other ways He has preserved and protected you?

Psalm 122

1 I was glad when they said unto me, Let us go into the house of the Lord.

2 Our feet shall stand within thy gates, O Jerusalem.

3 Jerusalem is builded as a city that is compact together:

4 Whither the tribes go up, the tribes of the Lord, unto the testimony of Israel, to give thanks unto the name of the Lord.

5 For there are set thrones of judgment, the thrones of the house of David.

6 Pray for the peace of Jerusalem: they shall prosper that love thee.

7 Peace be within thy walls, and prosperity within thy palaces.

8 For my brethren and companions' sakes, I will now say, Peace be within thee.

9 Because of the house of the Lord our God I will seek thy good.

Psalm 123

1 Unto thee lift I up mine eyes, O thou that dwellest in the heavens.

2 Behold, as the eyes of servants look unto the hand of their masters, and as the eyes of a maiden unto the hand of her mistress; so our eyes wait upon the Lord our God, until that he have mercy upon us.

3 Have mercy upon us, O Lord, have mercy upon us: for we are exceedingly filled with contempt.

4 Our soul is exceedingly filled with the scorning of those that are at ease, and with the contempt of the proud.

For Your Information

"The tribes of the Lord": the twelve tribes of Israel, from the twelve sons of Jacob (Genesis 29–30; 48:22).

"Thrones of the house of David": Jerusalem is the royal city, where the kings of David's line established their government.

"The hand of their masters": The servants look to God for direction, provision, and mercy.

"Those that are at ease": complacent ones, who deny God.

Psalm 122

As the pilgrims head for Jerusalem to worship, David rejoices in the city, both as the site of the temple and the place where Israel's government resides. He delights in the city for the first five verses.

The last verses are a prayer for Jerusalem's peace, prosperity, and safety. As His people meet God there, the psalmist prays for peace, so the worship of the Lord may continue.

- Jerusalem has always been a special place to believers. How is it special to you? Since Christians no longer need a special city in which to worship, what has become important?

Psalm 123

An unknown psalmist lifts his eyes to God, humbly looking to him for all he needs and seeking mercy. Unbelievers have looked at the faithful contemptuously, and the psalmist's soul is filled to overflowing with the mockery of those who deny God, so he looks to God for help.

- Are those who mock believers right—is it foolish to believe in God? What would the psalmist say about that, based on what you have read in previous psalms? Who do unbelievers look to for help? Where will that lead them?

Psalm 124

1 If it had not been the Lord who was on our side, now may Israel say;

2 If it had not been the Lord who was on our side, when men rose up against us:

3 Then they had swallowed us up quick, when their wrath was kindled against us:

4 Then the waters had overwhelmed us, the stream had gone over our soul:

5 Then the proud waters had gone over our soul.

6 Blessed be the Lord, who hath not given us as a prey to their teeth.

7 Our soul is escaped as a bird out of the snare of the fowlers: the snare is broken, and we are escaped.

8 Our help is in the name of the Lord, who made heaven and earth.

Psalm 125

1 They that trust in the Lord shall be as mount Zion, which cannot be removed, but abideth for ever.

2 As the mountains are round about Jerusalem, so the Lord is round about his people from henceforth even for ever.

3 For the rod of the wicked shall not rest upon the lot of the righteous; lest the righteous put forth their hands unto iniquity.

4 Do good, O Lord, unto those that be good, and to them that are upright in their hearts.

5 As for such as turn aside unto their crooked ways, the Lord shall lead them forth with the workers of iniquity: but peace shall be upon Israel.

For Your Information
"Quick": quickly.

"Waters. . .stream. . .proud waters": He compares Israel's enemies to powerful bodies of water, flooding out Israel.

"Given us as a prey to their teeth": allowed them to consume us. This compares the enemy to a hunting wild animal.

"As a bird out of the snare of the fowlers": like a bird that escaped a hunter's trap.

"Name": God's name identifies His nature. They trust in their powerful God.

"The Lord, who made heaven and earth": God the creator.

"Mount Zion": symbolic of the security of believers.

"Removed": moved.

"Rod": power.

"Shall not rest": shall not lie heavy on.

"The lot": the worldly portion.

"Crooked ways": ways of sin, not the straight path of God.

Psalm 124

Had God not protected Israel, David proclaims, the enemy would have swallowed up his nation. Pagan countries would have overwhelmed them, but God saved them. He praises the Lord, who enabled Israel to escape as a bird who got away because the trap was broken.

• Often the methods God uses to protect and preserve His people seem very ordinary, like the broken trap spoken of in this psalm. Has God used ordinary methods to do good things in you life? Did you recognize where they came from?

Psalm 125

Again a psalmist encourages Israel to trust in God, despite circumstances. God, who is as unmoveable as Zion (their place of worship) or the mountains around the city, is protecting them. Even when the wicked rule over them, they have power only for a time. God will not allow sinners to bring down the righteous by dragging them into sin.

He calls on God to do good to those who remain faithful to him and to give the unfaithful in Zion the reward of the wicked. In the end, Israel shall experience the peace God offers.

• Why are mountains a good picture of God's immutability? How does this word picture fall short of portraying God's nature? Can anything be as unchangeable as God?

Psalm 126

1 When the Lord turned again the captivity of Zion, we were like them that dream.

2 Then was our mouth filled with laughter, and our tongue with singing: then said they among the heathen, The Lord hath done great things for them.

3 The Lord hath done great things for us; whereof we are glad.

4 Turn again our captivity, O Lord, as the streams in the south.

5 They that sow in tears shall reap in joy.

6 He that goeth forth and weepeth, bearing precious seed, shall doubtless come again with rejoicing, bringing his sheaves with him.

Psalm 127

1 Except the Lord build the house, they labour in vain that build it: except the Lord keep the city, the watchman waketh but in vain.

2 It is vain for you to rise up early, to sit up late, to eat the bread of sorrows: for so he giveth his beloved sleep.

3 Lo, children are an heritage of the Lord: and the fruit of the womb is his reward.

4 As arrows are in the hand of a mighty man; so are children of the youth.

5 Happy is the man that hath his quiver full of them: they shall not be ashamed, but they shall speak with the enemies in the gate.

For Your Information

"Turned again the captivity of Zion": probably referring to the Babylonian exile, though this is not stated in the psalm or its attribution. The period of Israel's suffering for sin is ended, and God restores His people to their land.

"Turn again our captivity": restore all our captives, fully ending the exile, and complete the restoration of our nation by providing the security and blessings needed.

"In the south": in the Negev, where water appeared only in seasonal streams.

"Precious seed": for sowing crops.

"Except": unless.

"The house": the family.

"Keep": protect.

"The city": center of the government, symbolic of the nation.

"Bread of sorrows": food gotten by hard labor or eaten with sadness.

"Sleep": contentment. Another sign of God's blessing.

"Fruit of the womb": children.

"In the gate": in the courts. Court business usually took place at the gates of a city.

Psalm 126

This song of ascents most likely rejoices in the Jews' return from captivity in Babylon. Amazed at the turn of events, feeling as if their fondest dreams had been fulfilled, the people rejoice. Even the heathen (perhaps the people of Babylon, whom they left) recognize the hand of God in their restoration.

Verse 4 requests God to complete the blessing, flooding the nation with all its people and the blessings they still lacked, since they came back to a depleted city. Much work had yet to be done. But the unnamed psalmist believes their tears will be seed that brings a joyous harvest. Their time of great suffering is ended, and the work ahead will bring great benefit.

• God showed compassion when He ended the captivity and restored His people. He can also bring us joy, following a time of sorrow. Is it necessary for us to fall away from Him to enjoy such an experience? What blessings did Israel miss out on during her sin?

Psalm 127

The psalmist, either David or Solomon, offers wisdom for families, encouraging them to rely not on their own abilities and efforts, but on the

God who sustains them in all things. For where God does not guard a family or country, it will end in disaster. Instead of seeking to gain earthly wealth, the psalmist points the family to the blessings of children, whom God gives and enables to defend their father in the courts.

• Have you seen signs of God's watchful care over your family? If your family does not love Him, have you seen effects from the lack of that care? What steps do you need to take to implement the psalmist's advice in your family?

Psalm 128

1 Blessed is every one that feareth the Lord; that walketh in his ways.

2 For thou shalt eat the labour of thine hands: happy shalt thou be, and it shall be well with thee.

3 Thy wife shall be as a fruitful vine by the sides of thine house: thy children like olive plants round about thy table.

4 Behold, that thus shall the man be blessed that feareth the Lord.

5 The Lord shall bless thee out of Zion: and thou shalt see the good of Jerusalem all the days of thy life.

6 Yea, thou shalt see thy children's children, and peace upon Israel.

Psalm 129

1 Many a time have they afflicted me from my youth, may Israel now say:

2 Many a time have they afflicted me from my youth: yet they have not prevailed against me.

3 The plowers plowed upon my back: they made long their furrows.

4 The Lord is righteous: he hath cut asunder the cords of the wicked.

5 Let them all be confounded and turned back that hate Zion.

6 Let them be as the grass upon the housetops, which withereth afore it groweth up:

7 Wherewith the mower filleth not his hand; nor he that bindeth sheaves his bosom.

8 Neither do they which go by say, The blessing of the Lord be upon you: we bless you in the name of the Lord.

For Your Information

"Eat the labour of thy hands": Eat the food your labor provides you.

"By the sides of thine house": The wife is faithful, not straying.

"Olive plants": long-lived, luxuriant trees.

"Bless thee out of Zion": special blessings from the holy city.

"Peace upon Israel": The country shall live in peace.

"The plowers. . .their furrows": Their enemies have plowed them like fallow ground.

"Grass upon the housetops": like grass that seeds itself in an unfertile place.

"They which go by": passersby.

Psalm 128
Like the previous psalm, this speaks of the blessings of a life dependent on God and the joys it brings to the family. Those who live for God work to bring God's provision to the family. Happy relationships are theirs as the wife lives in peace with her husband and the children flourish.

God's blessings also reach their nation. Jerusalem prospers with such people living there, and the blessed ones see their grandchildren and peace in their country.

• How can God bless a nation filled with believing people? How can you take part in that blessing and pass it on?

Psalm 129
A prayer for the destruction of Israel's enemies, this orphan psalm poetically repeats a complaint of affliction in the first two verses, but the psalmist draws hope from the fact that his enemies have not prevailed. They have harmed Israel, but not destroyed the nation.

Calling on God's righteousness, the psalmist asks that the enemies be destroyed, as grass with no place for its roots to grow. Compared to the blessings given the faithful, they will reap destruction.

• What does a person need to do to be blessed by God? Can a Christian lose God's blessings? How? Can a nonbeliever gain them? How?

Psalm 130

1 Out of the depths have I cried unto thee, O Lord.

2 Lord, hear my voice: let thine ears be attentive to the voice of my supplications.

3 If thou, Lord, shouldest mark iniquities, O Lord, who shall stand?

4 But there is forgiveness with thee, that thou mayest be feared.

5 I wait for the Lord, my soul doth wait, and in his word do I hope.

6 My soul waiteth for the Lord more than they that watch for the morning: I say, more than they that watch for the morning.

7 Let Israel hope in the Lord: for with the Lord there is mercy, and with him is plenteous redemption.

8 And he shall redeem Israel from all his iniquities.

Psalm 131

1 Lord, my heart is not haughty, nor mine eyes lofty: neither do I exercise myself in great matters, or in things too high for me.

2 Surely I have behaved and quieted myself, as a child that is weaned of his mother: my soul is even as a weaned child.

3 Let Israel hope in the Lord from henceforth and for ever.

For Your Information

"Depths": of affliction, whether sin or a physical one.

"Shouldest mark iniquities": should count our sins against us.

"Waiteth for the Lord": with expectation.

"Plenteous": plentiful.

"Lofty": prideful.

"Exercise": involve, meddle with.

"Weaned child": a young, dependent child, somewhat beyond infancy.

Psalm 130

In this penitential orphan psalm, the psalmist cries out to God from a place of desperate trouble and asks Him to hear. He understands God's holiness cannot tolerate sin, but rejoices that He has not held sin against those who trust in Him. Awe for God comes from the experience of His forgiveness.

Trustingly, the psalmist waits for God to act, more confident than those who wait to end a night watch. The Creator who made night and day will surely keep His covenant promises. Redemption is not far off.

• When you are in the depths of trouble are you confident God will answer your prayers? Why? If He does not respond quickly, can you still trust He has heard? What does this psalm tell you about God's nature? His care for you?

Psalm 131

Following a psalm of repentance, these verses portray an orphan psalmist's complete trust in God. He is not looking to involve himself in great things, but to relax completely in faith, as a child relaxes in His mother's arms.

The final verse calls on Israel to follow his example and depend wholly on God.

• To do great things for God, is it necessary to hold a high position in the church, government, or business? How can you know what God is calling you to do? What role does trust play in that knowledge?

Psalm 132

1 Lord, remember David, and all his afflictions:

2 How he sware unto the Lord, and vowed unto the mighty God of Jacob;

3 Surely I will not come into the tabernacle of my house, nor go up into my bed;

4 I will not give sleep to mine eyes, or slumber to mine eyelids,

5 Until I find out a place for the Lord, an habitation for the mighty God of Jacob.

6 Lo, we heard of it at Ephratah: we found it in the fields of the wood.

7 We will go into his tabernacles: we will worship at his footstool.

8 Arise, O Lord, into thy rest; thou, and the ark of thy strength.

9 Let thy priests be clothed with righteousness; and let thy saints shout for joy.

10 For thy servant David's sake turn not away the face of thine anointed.

11 The Lord hath sworn in truth unto David; he will not turn from it; Of the fruit of thy body will I set upon thy throne.

12 If thy children will keep my covenant and my testimony that I shall teach them, their children shall also sit upon thy throne for evermore.

13 For the Lord hath chosen Zion; he hath desired it for his habitation.

14 This is my rest for ever: here will I dwell; for I have desired it.

15 I will abundantly bless her provision: I will satisfy her poor with bread.

16 I will also clothe her priests with salvation: and her saints shall shout aloud for joy.

17 There will I make the horn of David to bud: I have ordained a lamp for mine anointed.

18 His enemies will I clothe with shame: but upon himself shall his crown flourish.

For Your Information

"Habitation": the temple.

"Ephratah": region around Bethlehem, where the ark of the covenant lay (1 Samuel 7:1).

"Fields of the wood": Kiriath Jearim.

"Footstool": symbolic of the connection between heaven and earth. God sits upon His throne, with his feet on His footstool. Some commentators see this as being the ark of the covenant.

"Ark of thy strength": The ark symbolizes God's rule over Israel.

"Clothed with righteousness": The priests' ministry will show forth God's righteousness.

"The horn of David to bud": symbolic of the king's expanding power.

"Lamp": an ever-burning symbol of David's continual line of kings.

Psalm 132

Another orphan psalm, possibly written by Solomon or one of David's line of kings, asks God to continue David's line of rulers.

The first seven verses ask God to remember David and recount his concern for bringing the ark of the covenant into Jerusalem. Verses 3–4 use hyperbole, a form of exaggeration, to emphasize David's concern for God's ark. He would not rest until he cared for the ark. He sought it out and brought it to Jerusalem. Verses 8–10 are a prayer for the ark, as it comes to the city.

The rest of the psalm concerns God's covenant with David (2 Samuel 7:16), that an heir of his body would remain on Israel's throne. This promise comes with a condition: It will happen as long as Israel's kings keep the covenant. Though they were not faithful, God was. Jesus, who came from the line of David, eternally fulfills these prophecies. He is the horn and lamp, the final king in whom the crown flourishes.

• Israel did not remain faithful. Would it have been fair for God to end the covenant at that point? What does God's response tell you about Him? About His people?

WEEK TWELVE

Introduction

The beginning of this week completes the songs of ascents, which end with Psalm 134. Psalm 135 begins a short collection of orphan psalms, lasting through Psalm 137.

Following that is the final collection of psalms of David, from 138 through 145. In Psalms 140 and 141 the king uses unusual imagery, repeatedly mentioning body parts. Nowhere else in the Old Testament are these words used.

Psalm 146, which appears in this study out of order, begins and ends with "hallelujah," as do all the psalms following it, an appropriate way to end the book of Psalms, which have glorified God over and over again.

Psalm 133

1 Behold, how good and how pleasant it is for brethren to dwell together in unity!

2 It is like the precious ointment upon the head, that ran down upon the beard, even Aaron's beard: that went down to the skirts of his garments;

3 As the dew of Hermon, and as the dew that descended upon the mountains of Zion: for there the Lord commanded the blessing, even life for evermore.

Psalm 134

1 Behold, bless ye the Lord, all ye servants of the Lord, which by night stand in the house of the Lord.

2 Lift up your hands in the sanctuary, and bless the Lord.

3 The Lord that made heaven and earth bless thee out of Zion.

For Your Information

"Precious ointment. . .Aaron's beard": When he was made high priest, Aaron was anointed with oil, symbolic of his consecration to the position (Exodus 29:7) and the work of the Holy Spirit in and through him.

"Dew of Hermon": Mount Hermon's snow-covered mountains provided the main source of water for the Jordan River. If its precipitation were on Zion, the city would become extremely fertile.

"By night": those on duty during the night (1 Chronicles 9:33).

"Lift up your hands": a sign of praise.

Psalm 133

This psalm attributed to David rejoices in the unity of brethren. Some have connected this with the events in 2 Samuel 5, when David was made king over all Israel, though this is not specified in the superscription.

The psalmist compares brotherly agreement to the extravagant anointing Aaron received with holy oil. God provides powerful, generous blessings on His people whose relationships reflect His love. Like the precipitation Mount Hermon gives to Jerusalem, the Lord floods His people with good things, including eternal life with Him.

• Has knowing God changed your relationships with people? How? Can He help with relationships that still seem difficult? Have you brought them before Him and followed His way?

Psalm 134

In this, the last of the songs of ascents, the servants of God are called on to remain faithful to their duty for the night, to praise God. A priest ends the psalm with a blessing.

• How many people in your church remain consistently faithful in fulfilling their work for God? Have you made a point of thanking your pastor and other leaders for their faithfulness to you and the congregation? Perhaps now is the time to do so.

Psalm 135

1 Praise ye the Lord. Praise ye the name of the Lord; praise him, O ye servants of the Lord.

2 Ye that stand in the house of the Lord, in the courts of the house of our God.

3 Praise the Lord; for the Lord is good: sing praises unto his name; for it is pleasant.

4 For the Lord hath chosen Jacob unto himself, and Israel for his peculiar treasure.

5 For I know that the Lord is great, and that our Lord is above all gods.

6 Whatsoever the Lord pleased, that did he in heaven, and in earth, in the seas, and all deep places.

7 He causeth the vapours to ascend from the ends of the earth; he maketh lightnings for the rain; he bringeth the wind out of his treasuries.

8 Who smote the firstborn of Egypt, both of man and beast.

9 Who sent tokens and wonders into the midst of thee, O Egypt, upon Pharaoh, and upon all his servants.

10 Who smote great nations, and slew mighty kings;

11 Sihon king of the Amorites, and Og king of Bashan, and all the kingdoms of Canaan:

12 And gave their land for an heritage, an heritage unto Israel his people.

13 Thy name, O Lord, endureth for ever; and thy memorial, O Lord, throughout all generations.

14 For the Lord will judge his people, and he will repent himself concerning his servants.

15 The idols of the heathen are silver and gold, the work of men's hands.

16 They have mouths, but they speak not; eyes have they, but they see not;

17 They have ears, but they hear not; neither is there any breath in their mouths.

18 They that make them are like unto them: so is every one that trusteth in them.

19 Bless the Lord, O house of Israel: bless the Lord, O house of Aaron:

20 Bless the Lord, O house of Levi: ye that fear the Lord, bless the Lord.

21 Blessed be the Lord out of Zion, which dwelleth at Jerusalem. Praise ye the Lord.

For Your Information

"Peculiar": set apart, special.

"Vapours": clouds.

"Smote the firstborn of Egypt": a reference to the last plague God visited on Egypt (Exodus 11–12).

"Tokens": signs.

"Sihon king of the Amorites. . .kings of Canaan": Before the Jews came to the Promised Land, these kings held the land that became Israel.

"Heritage": inheritance.

Psalm 135

Beginning and ending with *hallelujah*, this orphan psalm calls the priests and Levites to praise Him for His goodness to Israel, His chosen people.

Verses 5–14 describe God's power and judgments, including creation; the final plague against Egypt, which caused Pharaoh to free Israel; and the conquering of the Promised Land. The people of Israel thank God for all He has done for them.

Verses 15–18 descry the idols of the pagan nations, who are not real and cannot do the works of God. Trust in them is useless.

In the final three verses, all His people praise God. In comparison to those who worship silver and gold, theirs is a living God.

• God has chosen you, if you have trusted in Him. What powerful things has He done that you need to praise Him for? What wrongs has He helped you avoid that you can thank Him for?

Psalm 136

1 O give thanks unto the Lord; for he is good: for his mercy endureth for ever.

2 O give thanks unto the God of gods: for his mercy endureth for ever.

3 O give thanks to the Lord of lords: for his mercy endureth for ever.

4 To him who alone doeth great wonders: for his mercy endureth for ever.

5 To him that by wisdom made the heavens: for his mercy endureth for ever.

6 To him that stretched out the earth above the waters: for his mercy endureth for ever.

7 To him that made great lights: for his mercy endureth for ever:

8 The sun to rule by day: for his mercy endureth for ever:

9 The moon and stars to rule by night: for his mercy endureth for ever.

10 To him that smote Egypt in their firstborn: for his mercy endureth for ever:

11 And brought out Israel from among them: for his mercy endureth for ever:

12 With a strong hand, and with a stretched out arm: for his mercy endureth for ever.

13 To him which divided the Red sea into parts: for his mercy endureth for ever:

14 And made Israel to pass through the midst of it: for his mercy endureth for ever:

15 But overthrew Pharaoh and his host in the Red sea: for his mercy endureth for ever.

16 To him which led his people through the wilderness: for his mercy endureth for ever.

17 To him which smote great kings: for his mercy endureth for ever:

18 And slew famous kings: for his mercy endureth for ever:

19 Sihon king of the Amorites: for his mercy endureth for ever:

20 And Og the king of Bashan: for his mercy endureth for ever:

21 And gave their land for an heritage: for his mercy endureth for ever:

22 Even an heritage unto Israel his servant: for his mercy endureth for ever.

23 Who remembered us in our low estate: for his mercy endureth for ever:

24 And hath redeemed us from our enemies: for his mercy endureth for ever.

25 Who giveth food to all flesh: for his mercy endureth for ever.

26 O give thanks unto the God of heaven: for his mercy endureth for ever.

For Your Information

"God of gods. . .Lord of lords": titles indicating God's supremacy.

"Low estate": captivity.

"God of heaven": a Persian title for God used in Ezra, Nehemiah, and Daniel, to differentiate the Lord from idols.

Psalm 136

Praise for God's mercy to His people is the focus of this orphan psalm that repeats the phrase "for his mercy endureth forever" in each verse. It may have been used in worship to be sung in two parts, with a leader taking the first part and a choir or the people responding with the refrain.

The first three verses call worshipers to give thanks to God, while the following ones describe many causes for thankfulness. Verses 4–9 speak of His works as the Creator, who made all parts of the universe; verses 10–16 recount the salvation of God's people in the Exodus and the journey to the Promised Land; while verses 17–22 outline the Lord's empowerment of His people to take the land He designed for them.

The last verses recount God's blessings in more general terms and call on them again to give thanks.

• Can you give a testimony to the mercy God has offered you as He saved you and gave you new life in Him? Share these truths with someone else, too.

Psalm 137

1 By the rivers of Babylon, there we sat down, yea, we wept, when we remembered Zion.

2 We hanged our harps upon the willows in the midst thereof.

3 For there they that carried us away captive required of us a song; and they that wasted us required of us mirth, saying, Sing us one of the songs of Zion.

4 How shall we sing the Lord's song in a strange land?

5 If I forget thee, O Jerusalem, let my right hand forget her cunning.

6 If I do not remember thee, let my tongue cleave to the roof of my mouth; if I prefer not Jerusalem above my chief joy.

7 Remember, O Lord, the children of Edom in the day of Jerusalem; who said, Rase it, rase it, even to the foundation thereof.

8 O daughter of Babylon, who art to be destroyed; happy shall he be, that rewardeth thee as thou hast served us.

9 Happy shall he be, that taketh and dasheth thy little ones against the stones.

Psalm 138

1 I will praise thee with my whole heart: before the gods will I sing praise unto thee.

2 I will worship toward thy holy temple, and praise thy name for thy lovingkindness and for thy truth: for thou hast magnified thy word above all thy name.

3 In the day when I cried thou answeredst me, and strengthenedst me with strength in my soul.

4 All the kings of the earth shall praise thee, O Lord, when they hear the words of thy mouth.

5 Yea, they shall sing in the ways of the Lord: for great is the glory of the Lord.

6 Though the Lord be high, yet hath he respect unto the lowly: but the proud he knoweth afar off.

7 Though I walk in the midst of trouble, thou wilt revive me: thou shalt stretch forth thine hand against the wrath of mine enemies, and thy right hand shall save me.

8 The Lord will perfect that which concerneth me: thy mercy, O Lord, endureth for ever: forsake not the works of thine own hands.

For Your Information

"Required of us mirth": demanded they sing joyful songs.

"How can we sing the songs of the Lord": Pagan people will not appreciate Israel's holy songs.

"Edom": Israel's enemies who rejoiced at the fall of Jerusalem.

"Rase": raze.

"Daughter of Bablyon": the Babylonian people.

"The gods": either pagan kings or the gods of their kingdoms.

"Worship toward": bow down toward.

"Magnified thy word": exalted your promises.

"Walk in the midst of trouble": live with trouble.

Psalm 137

In this orphan psalm the Israelites mourn their loss of their homeland during the Babylonian exile. Not only did a pagan people enslave them, their captors expected them to sing joyful songs of their land. But to sing of God before idolaters would dishonor God and their city.

The psalmist reminds God of Israel's enemies, including the nation of Edom, which wanted to see Jerusalem fall and be razed to its foundations. He prophesies that Babylon will fall and her people, even infants, will be destroyed.

• Despite their sorrows, the Israelites remembered Jerusalem and longed for it. What do you think they really desired? How does this psalm show that? When you are in trouble, do you respond as they did?

Psalm 138

David publicly praises God for His help, for He has kept His promises by responding and giving the king strength. Because He is so glorious, David calls all kings to worship Him.

This holy God cares for the lowly person while remaining distant from the proud one. In the final two verses, David speaks of his own experience in this regard and thanks Him for His mercy.

- What is lovingkindness? (You may want to look this word up in a dictionary.) How does God show it to people? How has it affected your life?

Psalm 139

1 O Lord, thou hast searched me, and known me.

2 Thou knowest my downsitting and mine uprising, thou understandest my thought afar off.

3 Thou compassest my path and my lying down, and art acquainted with all my ways.

4 For there is not a word in my tongue, but, lo, O Lord, thou knowest it altogether.

5 Thou hast beset me behind and before, and laid thine hand upon me.

6 Such knowledge is too wonderful for me; it is high, I cannot attain unto it.

7 Whither shall I go from thy spirit? or whither shall I flee from thy presence?

8 If I ascend up into heaven, thou art there: if I make my bed in hell, behold, thou art there.

9 If I take the wings of the morning, and dwell in the uttermost parts of the sea;

10 Even there shall thy hand lead me, and thy right hand shall hold me.

11 If I say, Surely the darkness shall cover me; even the night shall be light about me.

12 Yea, the darkness hideth not from thee; but the night shineth as the day: the darkness and the light are both alike to thee.

13 For thou hast possessed my reins: thou hast covered me in my mother's womb.

14 I will praise thee; for I am fearfully and wonderfully made: marvellous are thy works; and that my soul knoweth right well.

15 My substance was not hid from thee, when I was made in secret, and curiously wrought in the lowest parts of the earth.

16 Thine eyes did see my substance, yet being unperfect; and in thy book all my members were written, which in continuance were fashioned, when as yet there was none of them.

17 How precious also are thy thoughts unto me, O God! how great is the sum of them!

18 If I should count them, they are more in number than the sand: when I awake, I am still with thee.

19 Surely thou wilt slay the wicked, O God: depart from me therefore, ye bloody men.

20 For they speak against thee wickedly, and thine enemies take thy name in vain.

21 Do not I hate them, O Lord, that hate thee? and am not I grieved with those that rise up against thee?

22 I hate them with perfect hatred: I count them mine enemies.

23 Search me, O God, and know my heart: try me, and know my thoughts:

24 And see if there be any wicked way in me, and lead me in the way everlasting.

For Your Information

"Compassest": encompassed.

"Beset": surrounded

"Possessed my reins": created my innermost parts (literally, kidneys).

"Covered me": hid me.

"Thy book": Your divine record book.

"Bloody men": those who oppose God and seek to kill others.

"Perfect": absolute.

"The way everlasting": the eternal path of godliness.

Psalm 139

David penned this psalm of God's intimate love for and rule over His created beings. The psalmist praises the Lord who created him and knows his every action and thought, down to his words even before they leave his mouth. God surrounds David with His amazing capacity to know all.

Though he asks hypothetical questions about escaping God, of course, there is no avoiding Him. No matter where the psalmist goes, God will be there, directing his life. After all, God created the deepest parts of his inner being. David feels awed at God's ability to put together life so perfectly and in such detail. Before he lived a day, God knew every moment of his life.

Considering God's power over his life, David is amazed. God's thoughts (and by implication the actions that come from them) are too many to count. They constantly surround the psalmist.

He calls on God to slay those who do not accept His love and personally rejects them for their ungodliness. David has so thoroughly associated with God that he even shares His enemies. He ends by asking God to search out any sin in him and lead him instead into godliness.

- When God searches our thoughts and hearts, what does He find? What response did the psalmist have? What does our response need to be? If God is not searching your heart, what could that mean? How can you make things right?

- How does it make you feel to understand that God knows all you do, even before you do it? Will it make you mindful of the need to avoid sin? How much you need His help to do that?

Psalm 140

1 Deliver me, O Lord, from the evil man: preserve me from the violent man;

2 Which imagine mischiefs in their heart; continually are they gathered together for war.

3 They have sharpened their tongues like a serpent; adders' poison is under their lips. Selah.

4 Keep me, O Lord, from the hands of the wicked; preserve me from the violent man; who have purposed to overthrow my goings.

5 The proud have hid a snare for me, and cords; they have spread a net by the wayside; they have set gins for me. Selah.

6 I said unto the Lord, Thou art my God: hear the voice of my supplications, O Lord.

7 O God the Lord, the strength of my salvation, thou hast covered my head in the day of battle.

8 Grant not, O Lord, the desires of the wicked: further not his wicked device; lest they exalt themselves. Selah.

9 As for the head of those that compass me about, let the mischief of their own lips cover them.

10 Let burning coals fall upon them: let them be cast into the fire; into deep pits, that they rise not up again.

11 Let not an evil speaker be established in the earth: evil shall hunt the violent man to overthrow him.

12 I know that the Lord will maintain the cause of the afflicted, and the right of the poor.

13 Surely the righteous shall give thanks unto thy name: the upright shall dwell in thy presence.

For Your Information

"Imagine": devise.

"Sharpened their tongues like a serpent": a picture of the cunning nature of his enemies.

"Gins": snares for catching game.

"Covered my head": protected me. David had experienced this before, in the midst of warfare. Now he asks for it in the face of a different kind of attack.

"Device": plan.

"Burning coals": a picture of destruction falling on them, perhaps a reference to the destruction of Sodom and Gomorrah (Genesis 19).

"Evil speaker": slanderer.

Psalm 140

Psalms 140–145 are all written by David. Possibly all come from the same period in his life. Psalm 142 was written "when he was in the cave," so these six psalms could have been penned when he fled from Saul. In Psalm 140 David prays for deliverance from slanderous enemies, which could certainly have been his experience at that time. No matter what the situation he wrote the psalms in, they contain valuable truths.

David starts with a request that God intervene in the situation between him and his malicious enemies (verses 1–3). The next two verses request protection from these violent men who have set many kinds of traps for him, to be certain they will cause his downfall.

In verses 6–8 David cries out to God for help and trusts it will come from the Lord, who guards him. He asks God to frustrate his enemies' evil plans, since they will not glorify Him. The following verses imagine the harm God will cause his enemies, perhaps even into eternity, as the language of flames and pits in verse 10 seems to imply.

David ends with a firm assurance that God will do right by the afflicted and poor. Those whom God has saved and who follow His will shall live with Him for eternity.

• Read Exodus 34:6; Deuteronomy 32:4; Psalm 51:6; 119:160; Proverbs 10:18; John 1:14 Why is slander so offensive to God? What does He expect of His people in this regard?

Psalm 141

1 Lord, I cry unto thee: make haste unto me; give ear unto my voice, when I cry unto thee.

2 Let my prayer be set forth before thee as incense; and the lifting up of my hands as the evening sacrifice.

3 Set a watch, O Lord, before my mouth; keep the door of my lips.

4 Incline not my heart to any evil thing, to practise wicked works with men that work iniquity: and let me not eat of their dainties.

5 Let the righteous smite me; it shall be a kindness: and let him reprove me; it shall be an excellent oil, which shall not break my head: for yet my prayer also shall be in their calamities.

6 When their judges are overthrown in stony places, they shall hear my words; for they are sweet.

7 Our bones are scattered at the grave's mouth, as when one cutteth and cleaveth wood upon the earth.

8 But mine eyes are unto thee, O God the Lord: in thee is my trust; leave not my soul destitute.

9 Keep me from the snares which they have laid for me, and the gins of the workers of iniquity.

10 Let the wicked fall into their own nets, whilst that I withal escape.

Psalm 146

1 Praise ye the Lord. Praise the Lord, O my soul.

2 While I live will I praise the Lord: I will sing praises unto my God while I have any being.

3 Put not your trust in princes, nor in the son of man, in whom there is no help.

4 His breath goeth forth, he returneth to his earth; in that very day his thoughts perish.

5 Happy is he that hath the God of Jacob for his help, whose hope is in the Lord his God:

6 Which made heaven, and earth, the sea, and all that therein is: which keepeth truth for ever:

7 Which executeth judgment for the oppressed: which giveth food to the hungry. The Lord looseth the prisoners:

8 The Lord openeth the eyes of the blind: the Lord raiseth them

that are bowed down: the Lord loveth the righteous:

9 The Lord preserveth the strangers; he relieveth the fatherless and widow: but the way of the wicked he turneth upside down.

10 The Lord shall reign for ever, even thy God, O Zion, unto all generations. Praise ye the Lord.

For Your Information

"Make haste unto me": hurry to me.

"Give ear": listen.

"As incense": incense symbolizes prayer.

"Practise wicked works": do evil deeds.

"In their calamities": against their wicked actions.

"Overthrown in stony places": thrown over a cliff, a punishment in the biblical era (see Luke 4:29).

"The son of man": mortal man. Jesus used this title to describe Himself, but in Him there *is* help because He is also God.

"His breath goeth forth, he returneth to his earth": He stops breathing and is buried.

"Looseth the prisoners": a reference to the Exodus and end of the Babylonian exile.

Psalm 141

Desperate, David prays and asks God to hear. Aware of his own sinful tendencies, he admits God must help him avoid evil. He accepts the correction of the righteous, whose criticism would be helpful for his soul, but prays against his wicked critics. He will be heard when those who wrongfully judge him are destroyed and their bones scattered.

The psalmist ends by trusting God with his soul and for protection from the snares of the enemy. He hopes they will fall into their own traps, while he escapes.

• Name three things David prays for here. What do they show about his heart? His needs? His God? When you face a desperate situation, how can prayer help?

Psalm 146

Another orphan psalm calls believers to worship the Lord instead of trusting in even the most powerful leader. For all people die, and their thoughts with them.

In contrast, joy comes to those who trust in God, the Creator, who looks out for the downtrodden but undoes the plans of the wicked. Trust in the Lord is wise, because He reigns forever.

• How do you know whom you trust in? Is your trust wise?

WEEK THIRTEEN

Introduction

As we come to the end of the Psalms, we finish the last group connected with David and move on to a set of praises that end Psalms with a loud "Rejoice!" David's psalms explore some of the difficulties of faith, but in the last psalms, we turn to pure delight in the powerful God of our salvation.

Each of the last five psalms (one of which we have already studied) begins and ends with "hallelujah." The implication may be that, just like the psalms, our lives should be surrounded with praise.

As we end this study of the Psalms, it is time to think about the things learned here. David has been an excellent teacher, along with the other psalmists. But we have learned more than simply words in which to praise God. The entire Christian life has been depicted here. Through Israel's king, we've seen what it means to be a person of faith. We've seen David struggling within himself when his life seemed incredibly difficult or even appeared about to end. We've seen him trust God, despite the doubt that plagued him, because of his life situation. Though his enemies were stronger than the king, God did not desert him. No one who came against David was more powerful than God.

But the Christian life is not only about struggle. As the Psalms show us, it also brings incredible joy. We've heard all the psalmists fill the earth with praise for the works God has done, either in Israel's past or just a second ago in their lives.

Because our lives also have seen both trial and joy, we relate to the psalmists. God has done wonderful things for us too, whether in our past or the history of our church or country. Also like the biblical psalmists, we can praise Him for the care He has shown for us and the guidance He has given.

We, too, can raise a psalm to our God, whose salvation we have experienced through His Son, Jesus Christ.

Psalm 142

1 I cried unto the Lord with my voice; with my voice unto the Lord did I make my supplication.

2 I poured out my complaint before him; I shewed before him my trouble.

3 When my spirit was overwhelmed within me, then thou knewest my path. In the way wherein I walked have they privily laid a snare for me.

4 I looked on my right hand, and beheld, but there was no man that would know me: refuge failed me; no man cared for my soul.

5 I cried unto thee, O Lord: I said, Thou art my refuge and my portion in the land of the living.

6 Attend unto my cry; for I am brought very low: deliver me from my persecutors; for they are stronger than I.

7 Bring my soul out of prison, that I may praise thy name: the righteous shall compass me about; for thou shalt deal bountifully with me.

For Your Information

"Poured out my complaint": This is not an objection, but meditation on his situation. He freely shares his concerns with God.

"Right hand": a protector's position.

"My portion": the one who sustains him.

"Prison": He has been surrounded by his enemies and afflicted by their presence.

Psalm 142

Surrounded by his enemies, taking refuge in a cave (1 Samuel 22:1 or 24:3), in prayer David cries out to God for help. His enemies have laid traps for him again, but though he feels wrapped in gloom, David reminds himself that God still knows his path. Though he may walk in confusion, the darkness of his situation cannot overwhelm God.

No man cared for David and his situation. No one offered him protection, refuge or spiritual help. Driven to God by his circumstances, the psalmist looks to Him for protection. Admitting that his enemies are more powerful than he, the anointed king turns to his anointer for freedom from his enemies and his situation. He trusts that in time he will praise God, surrounded not by enemies but by the righteous. God will be bountiful.

- When you feel concerned about a problem in your life, do you pour out your complaint to God, or do you avoid Him? What results have you gotten from doing each? Which is better to do? How can you make certain you bring your concerns to God?

- When you face difficult circumstances, do they drive you closer to God or farther away? How does your reaction to trouble relate to your response? When you rely on God instead of complaining, how does it change things?

Psalm 143

1 Hear my prayer, O Lord, give ear to my supplications: in thy faithfulness answer me, and in thy righteousness.

2 And enter not into judgment with thy servant: for in thy sight shall no man living be justified.

3 For the enemy hath persecuted my soul; he hath smitten my life down to the ground; he hath made me to dwell in darkness, as those that have been long dead.

4 Therefore is my spirit overwhelmed within me; my heart within me is desolate.

5 I remember the days of old; I meditate on all thy works; I muse on the work of thy hands.

6 I stretch forth my hands unto thee: my soul thirsteth after thee, as a thirsty land. Selah.

7 Hear me speedily, O Lord: my spirit faileth: hide not thy face from me, lest I be like unto them that go down into the pit.

8 Cause me to hear thy lovingkindness in the morning; for in thee do I trust: cause me to know the way wherein I should walk; for I lift up my soul unto thee.

9 Deliver me, O Lord, from mine enemies: I flee unto thee to hide me.

10 Teach me to do thy will; for thou art my God: thy spirit is good; lead me into the land of uprightness.

11 Quicken me, O Lord, for thy name's sake: for thy righteousness' sake bring my soul out of trouble.

12 And of thy mercy cut off mine enemies, and destroy all them that afflict my soul: for I am thy servant.

For Your Information

"Give ear": listen.

"Enter not into judgment": do not judge me.

"Dwell in darkness": physically, to live in a cave or, spiritually, to live as one with no delight in life.

"Stretch forth my hands": seeking help.

"Thirsteth": In a time of spiritual dryness, he longs for God, as a parched land needs rain.

"The pit": the grave.

"Lift up": offer up.

"Quicken me": enliven my spirit.

Psalm 143

In this penitential psalm, David humbly asks God's aid against his enemies. Aware of his own sinfulness, he reminds God of His covenant promises concerning faithfulness and righteousness and asks Him not to judge Him. Though David's frail attempts at faith are not perfect enough for a holy Lord, God had agreed not to condemn those who would covenant with Him to be His people. He could do that because Jesus' sacrifice (which the animal sacrifices in the Old Testament prefigured) would take the place of the death sinners deserved (see Romans 6:23). In His death on the cross, Jesus took God's wrath for all people, and in his compassion, God forgave all who trusted in His Son. Aware of his own sinfulness and God's holiness, David appeals to Him, knowing that under his own power he cannot achieve justification.

Verses 3–4 outline David's complaint against his enemies, whose continual attack has discouraged him. But as he remembers God's works in the past, the psalmist turns to Him for help. Weakening, he entreats God not to fail him, or he will be like those who die. Instead he seeks God's lovingkindness, because he trusts and seeks to obey Him.

David does not end with a request for God's help. He offers God his whole life and soul in return. Getting out of one tough situation is not enough. David wants to live entirely for God and experience His help and protection. He ends by affirming that he is God's servant.

• David wanted God's help. Why would he have reason to expect it? What was his attitude? What had he already done to make his request acceptable to God? What is he willing to do? What does this mean for people who want God's help but do not want to do anything in response?

Psalm 144

1 Blessed be the Lord my strength which teacheth my hands to war, and my fingers to fight:

2 My goodness, and my fortress; my high tower, and my deliverer; my shield, and he in whom I trust; who subdueth my people under me.

3 Lord, what is man, that thou takest knowledge of him! or the son of man, that thou makest account of him!

4 Man is like to vanity: his days are as a shadow that passeth away.

5 Bow thy heavens, O Lord, and come down: touch the mountains, and they shall smoke.

6 Cast forth lightning, and scatter them: shoot out thine arrows, and destroy them.

7 Send thine hand from above; rid me, and deliver me out of great waters, from the hand of strange children;

8 Whose mouth speaketh vanity, and their right hand is a right hand of falsehood.

9 I will sing a new song unto thee, O God: upon a psaltery and an instrument of ten strings will I sing praises unto thee.

10 It is he that giveth salvation unto kings: who delivereth David his servant from the hurtful sword.

11 Rid me, and deliver me from the hand of strange children, whose mouth speaketh vanity, and their right hand is a right hand of falsehood:

12 That our sons may be as plants grown up in their youth; that our daughters may be as corner stones, polished after the similitude of a palace:

13 That our garners may be full, affording all manner of store: that our sheep may bring forth thousands and ten thousands in our streets:

14 That our oxen may be strong to labour; that there be no breaking in, nor going out; that there be no complaining in our streets.

15 Happy is that people, that is in such a case: yea, happy is that people, whose God is the Lord.

For Your Information

"Teacheth my hands to war": teaches me to fight.

"Like to vanity": like a profitless thing.

"They shall smoke": This fiery allusion shows God's power.

"Great waters": a threatening situation.

"Strange children": foreigners.

"Right hand": the hand used to swear to a covenant.

"Garners": storehouses, barns.

"Breaking in": into the city walls.

Psalm 144

Like Psalm 18, to which it is similar, this psalm of David praises his beloved God for helping him in battle and being his protector and deliverer. Aware of the fragility of all people, he is amazed that God cares for people, who are frivolous, frail beings, compared to Himself.

In verses 5–8 the king calls on his powerful Lord to come down in all His awesome strength and rescue him from earthly dangers and the lying foreign enemies who would have surrounded his nation. In response to this aid, he offers praise, acknowledging God's deliverance from those lying, covenant-breaking enemies.

When God provides this deliverance, it will have a powerful impact on Israel, whose children, crops, and animals will flourish. The people will be happy in their land. But even more, they will be happy because the Lord is their God.

• What brings more happiness, living in a prosperous country or having a close relationship with God? How are the two related? When you do not have one, does it necessarily mean you are missing the other?

Psalm 145

1 I will extol thee, my God, O king; and I will bless thy name for ever and ever.

2 Every day will I bless thee; and I will praise thy name for ever and ever.

3 Great is the Lord, and greatly to be praised; and his greatness is unsearchable.

4 One generation shall praise thy works to another, and shall declare thy mighty acts.

5 I will speak of the glorious honour of thy majesty, and of thy wondrous works.

6 And men shall speak of the might of thy terrible acts: and I will declare thy greatness.

7 They shall abundantly utter the memory of thy great goodness, and shall sing of thy righteousness.

8 The Lord is gracious, and full of compassion; slow to anger, and of great mercy.

9 The Lord is good to all: and his tender mercies are over all his works.

10 All thy works shall praise thee, O Lord; and thy saints shall bless thee.

11 They shall speak of the glory of thy kingdom, and talk of thy power;

12 To make known to the sons of men his mighty acts, and the glorious majesty of his kingdom.

13 Thy kingdom is an everlasting kingdom, and thy dominion endureth throughout all generations.

14 The Lord upholdeth all that fall, and raiseth up all those that be bowed down.

15 The eyes of all wait upon thee; and thou givest them their meat in due season.

16 Thou openest thine hand, and satisfiest the desire of every living thing.

17 The Lord is righteous in all his ways, and holy in all his works.

18 The Lord is nigh unto all them that call upon him, to all that call upon him in truth.

19 He will fulfil the desire of them that fear him: he also will hear

their cry, and will save them.

20 The Lord preserveth all them that love him: but all the wicked will he destroy.

21 My mouth shall speak the praise of the Lord: and let all flesh bless his holy name for ever and ever.

For Your Information

"Bless thy name": Since God's name reflects His nature, the psalmist is praising more than simply the word God is called by.

"Unsearchable": unfathomable. God's power is beyond human understanding.

"Terrible acts": awesome shows of power.

"Nigh": near.

"All flesh": all people.

Psalm 145

David begins this praise psalm by promising to extol God's name eternally. Calling others to join him in his joy, he foresees they will pass on the reasons to praise from one generation to the next.

David begins the praise time as he declares God's wonderful works in verses 5–7, then continues to describe His gracious character, while calling the saints to praise Him. Verses 14–16 describe God's faithfulness in providing for all who live, weak and strong. Verses 17–20 praise His righteousness and end with the psalmist's repeated call to all people to bless Him.

• How can you pass on the praise of God to another generation? Does it matter if you have children? If you do, what opportunities do you have to do this in your home? In church? Elsewhere?

• How many reasons does the psalmist give us to praise God? How have you experienced these?

Psalm 147

1 Praise ye the Lord: for it is good to sing praises unto our God; for it is pleasant; and praise is comely.

2 The Lord doth build up Jerusalem: he gathereth together the outcasts of Israel.

3 He healeth the broken in heart, and bindeth up their wounds.

4 He telleth the number of the stars; he calleth them all by their names.

5 Great is our Lord, and of great power: his understanding is infinite.

6 The Lord lifteth up the meek: he casteth the wicked down to the ground.

7 Sing unto the Lord with thanksgiving; sing praise upon the harp unto our God:

8 Who covereth the heaven with clouds, who prepareth rain for the earth, who maketh grass to grow upon the mountains.

9 He giveth to the beast his food, and to the young ravens which cry.

10 He delighteth not in the strength of the horse: he taketh not pleasure in the legs of a man.

11 The Lord taketh pleasure in them that fear him, in those that hope in his mercy.

12 Praise the Lord, O Jerusalem; praise thy God, O Zion.

13 For he hath strengthened the bars of thy gates; he hath blessed thy children within thee.

14 He maketh peace in thy borders, and filleth thee with the finest of the wheat.

15 He sendeth forth his commandment upon earth: his word runneth very swiftly.

16 He giveth snow like wool: he scattereth the hoarfrost like ashes.

17 He casteth forth his ice like morsels: who can stand before his cold?

18 He sendeth out his word, and melteth them: he causeth his wind to blow, and the waters flow.

19 He sheweth his word unto Jacob, his statutes and his judgments unto Israel.

20 He hath not dealt so with any nation: and as for his judgments, they have not known them. Praise ye the Lord.

For Your Information

"Comely": becoming.

"Build up. . .outcasts of Israel": a reference to the return of Israel from Babylon.

"To the ground": perhaps even to death.

"Strengthened the bars of thy gates": made the city's defenses strong.

"Sendeth out his word": gives the command.

"Sheweth his word unto Jacob. . .Israel": He reveals his truths to the people of Israel.

Psalm 147

Though some commentators believe this is a psalm of David, references that imply a date after the Babylonian exile seem to place it later, perhaps after Jerusalem's walls were rebuilt. No superscription describes the situation in which it was written.

The unnamed psalmist reminds us that praise for God is good, pleasant, and becoming to His people, following which he focuses on specific reasons for praise: He reminds them of God's compassion in returning them to their homeland and healing them, body and soul.

He continues to offer reasons for praise by picturing God's magnificence, compassion, and justice. Again he calls on the faithful to praise God, reminding them of His daily care in sending rain to water the land and provide food. But God's pleasure is not in these things, be they animal or human. He delights in those who love and serve Him.

The final call to praise is another reminder of God's blessings of protection and provision. The world has no choice but to obey this powerful Lord's commands concerning weather. But only to His people, not the nations around them has He revealed His Word. Indeed that is reason to praise God.

• God provides differently for people and other parts of creation. How does He provide for each? How does each benefit the other? What does this tell you about creation? How we should or should not treat our world?

- The church understands Israel to describe not only the Old Testament nation, but also the New Testament faithful in the church. How do the last two verses of this psalm relate to the Old Testament people? New Testament believers? What is the difference? What is the same?

Psalm 148

1 Praise ye the Lord. Praise ye the Lord from the heavens: praise him in the heights.

2 Praise ye him, all his angels: praise ye him, all his hosts.

3 Praise ye him, sun and moon: praise him, all ye stars of light.

4 Praise him, ye heavens of heavens, and ye waters that be above the heavens.

5 Let them praise the name of the Lord: for he commanded, and they were created.

6 He hath also stablished them for ever and ever: he hath made a decree which shall not pass.

7 Praise the Lord from the earth, ye dragons, and all deeps:

8 Fire, and hail; snow, and vapour; stormy wind fulfilling his word:

9 Mountains, and all hills; fruitful trees, and all cedars:

10 Beasts, and all cattle; creeping things, and flying fowl:

11 Kings of the earth, and all people; princes, and all judges of the earth:

12 Both young men, and maidens; old men, and children:

13 Let them praise the name of the Lord: for his name alone is excellent; his glory is above the earth and heaven.

14 He also exalteth the horn of his people, the praise of all his saints; even of the children of Israel, a people near unto him. Praise ye the Lord.

For Your Information

"From the heavens": The psalmist calls on the angels to praise God.

"In the heights": in the heavens.

"Heavens of heavens": the highest heavens, where God is.

"Shall not pass": will not end.

"Dragons": sea creatures.

"Fire": lightning.

"Vapours": clouds.

"Excellent": exalted.

"Horn of his people": either His anointed one or the power of Israel.

"Near to him": close to Him in love.

Psalm 148

In this orphan psalm, the praise begins in the heavens, with angels lifting up their voices in worship. Then the psalmist calls on the heavenly bodies to join their song, for the Lord God created them and upholds them with His power. His decree alone changes them.

Moving downward, the psalmist calls on the earth, down to the depths of the sea, to praise God. From the lightning and precipitation that falls to earth, the heights of the land, and all that inhabits the earth, he enjoins praise. All people, from the most powerful to the small child, should join in glorifying the one with power above all. They should praise the One who lifts up His people.

• Why does the psalmist call on everything, from the angels down through creation to worship God? What does this tell you about God and His glory? About creation? Why do His people have a special reason to praise?

Psalm 149

1 Praise ye the Lord. Sing unto the Lord a new song, and his praise in the congregation of saints.

2 Let Israel rejoice in him that made him: let the children of Zion be joyful in their King.

3 Let them praise his name in the dance: let them sing praises unto him with the timbrel and harp.

4 For the Lord taketh pleasure in his people: he will beautify the meek with salvation.

5 Let the saints be joyful in glory: let them sing aloud upon their beds.

6 Let the high praises of God be in their mouth, and a two-edged sword in their hand;

7 To execute vengeance upon the heathen, and punishments upon the people;

8 To bind their kings with chains, and their nobles with fetters of iron;

9 To execute upon them the judgment written: this honour have all his saints. Praise ye the Lord.

Psalm 150

1 Praise ye the Lord. Praise God in his sanctuary: praise him in the firmament of his power.

2 Praise him for his mighty acts: praise him according to his excellent greatness.

3 Praise him with the sound of the trumpet: praise him with the psaltery and harp.

4 Praise him with the timbrel and dance: praise him with stringed instruments and organs.

5 Praise him upon the loud cymbals: praise him upon the high sounding cymbals.

6 Let every thing that hath breath praise the Lord. Praise ye the Lord.

For Your Information

"New song": celebrating God's salvation and mercy.

"In the dance": a picture of great joy.

"Meek": humble, merciful.

"Upon their beds": a former place of sorrow (see Psalm 6).

"Two-edged sword": the kind of sword mainly used in Israel, which was sharp on both sides and effective for thrusting.

"In his sanctuary": on in His earthly temple.

"Firmament": heavens.

"Organ": pipe.

Psalm 149

Many new songs can be sung about God's salvation, as we discover more about it each day. Here the undesignated psalmist declares God's mercy anew. The first six verses make joyful praise, using the body and voice, as they praise the Lord who delights in them, too.

The last three verses describe their warfare against God's enemies, as they have the honor to serve Him.

• What does it mean to sing a new song? Does it happen once or many times in a Christian's life? What does it mean when Christians do not feel like singing a new song?

Psalm 150

Ending the series of hallelujah psalms begun in Psalm 146, this joyful orphan psalm is a fitting end for the psalter and may indeed have been written specifically to take that place.

"Praise" is the word constantly used in this psalm, since it appears at least once in each verse. In His temple, all are called to praise the Lord's greatness, shown forth in His firmament. Verses 3–5 specify various instruments with which praise goes forth, from the very loud to the very quiet.

The book of Psalms ends with a call to all living beings to praise God.

• Must worship be loud? Quiet? What does this psalm say? How do you think God defines real worship?